TODAY'S ROYAL NAVY IN COLOUR

Above: The image that usually springs to mind of the final stages of a submarine attack is of the captain viewing the target through the periscope. In modern warfare the aids in the conning tower have advanced considerably from the days of World War 2. Besides the basic image of the target, the periscope can provide information on its range. Also included are an image intensifier, a camera to record the image, and even thermal imaging equipment. This information, or images, can be transmitted to the Fire Control System or recorded for later analysis.

This edition specially published in 1996 for Greenwich Editions, Bibliophile House, 10 Blenheim Court, Brewery Road, London N7 9NT.

First published in the UK in 1995 by Arms & Amour (A Cassell imprint)

ISBN 0 86288 089 0

Printed and bound in Italy by Manfrini S.p.a. Calliano (TN)

ACKNOWLEDGEMENTS
I would like to thank the Captains, officers and ratings of the numerous ships, squadrons and establishments I have visited during the course of producing this book. While it is impossible to list everyone personally, I would like to thank the following who were instrumental in arranging many of the facilities. These include Leslie Burgess, Lorraine Coulton, Steve Dargan, CPO Al Campbell, Captain Esplin Jones, Captain Fanshawe, Commander Duncan Fergusson, 1/O David Gatenby, JenniferGriffiths, David Harris, David Healey, Tracy Shepherd-Jennings, Mark Steels and Juliet Summers. I would also like to thank my wife Julie, for her patience during the lengthy production of this book, and who together with my daughters Lucy and Loretta assisted me on some of the photo shoots.

Picture Credits
All the photographs in this book were taken by the author with the exception of the following: BAe, 132t, 103m; BAe SEMA, 105b; Alan Clements, 142b; FBM, 145; Ferranti, 26, 82, 93b; GEC-Marconi, 21 all, 65t, 109tl; Huntings, 181m; Lockheed, 14b; MoD, 11, 12, 13m, 14t, 15t, 16t, 17t, 18t, 18b, 22t, 23, 24/5, 36t, 50bl, 64b, 86t, 87b, 93t, 108b, 111m, 113b, 114, 116b, 118b, 119 both, 120b, 125bl, 129t, 130t, 135b, 144, 151b, 152, 154t, 154m, 156t, 156m, 156b, 157t, 158b, 159 all, 160, 161 both, 162, 163, 171b, 174b, 186t; Paxman Diesels, 108m; Henry Steel, 140m, 143b; Vosper, 107.

Contents

Below: It may appear peaceful, but when required the ship's company who have been thoroughly trained are ready to meet the threat – from wherever it comes!

TODAY'S
ROYAL NAVY
IN COLOUR

JEREMY FLACK

GREENWICH EDITIONS
NEW ORCHARD

Introduction

For an island, the control of the surrounding sea is of paramount importance. In the distant past, to prevent marauding warships from invading coastal towns. Today, to ensure the safe passage of merchant vessels to freely trade with other nations and to allow fishing fleets to harvest the seas unhindered are all good reasons for a strong naval force.

Great Britain has suffered on numerous occasions over the centuries past from attacks of one form or another from the Romans, Vikings, Saxons, French and Spanish. In more recent times the Germans during World War 1 and 2.

The embryo of today's Royal Navy can be traced back over 1,000 years when King Alfred established the idea of a King's Navy to stem the vicious Viking attacks. Eventually, to meet the threats small groups of ships was established at strategic location by the crown to provide a milit ary force.

From the 16th Century onwards, the developments in shipping and navigation provided a means of expansion of British influence. Voyages of discovery were constantly being conducted to the new world. Britain wasn't alone in this rush to discover the world. Amongst others there were the French,

Spanish and Dutch. As rich lands were discovered conflicts over them would ensue. The merchant ships returning home heavily laden with riches from these new worlds became targets for marauding pirates. Battles were fought for control of the seas with a combination of military and merchant vessels. During the battle to defeat the Spanish Armada 34 royal ships together with 100 merchant vessels were amassed.

Merchant ships had progressively becoming more heavily armed but this was not enough and specialist military ships evolved. The merchant ships retained a self defence capability while the fighting ships would provide an armed protection in potentially dangerous waters.

The Royal Navy was evolving into a disciplined and professional force. The principles of pay and procurement as well as structure and administration had been firmly established by Samuel Pepys by the time that he retired in 1659.

From the late 17th Century onwards the Royal Navy shared the dominance of the seas with the French. Numerous battles were fought for outright dominance. The Royal Navy was fundamental in the

Left: HMS *Victory* remains Flagship of C-in-C Naval Home Command.

Right: A *Trafalgar* Class hunter/ killer submarine commences a patrol from Devonport. Invitations to tender have been issued for an additional batch of three boats and an option on a further two.

establishment and protection of the British Empire.

The advent of the iron ships and coal power saw the end of the fine wooden sail ships. The lead up to World War 1 saw the introduction of powerful warships with impressive firepower. The action at Jutland with the German Fleet in 1916 saw the demise of the battles at sea with large numbers of warship. Soon to rear their head were the German 'U-Boats' or submarines.

Initially these were crude boats but they soon the submarines were posing an unacceptably high threat to British and Allied shipping. Also entering the arena at this time were aircraft although the early models were very flimsy, it wasn't long before effective flying machines were taking to the air.

During World War 2 both the submarine and the aircraft were dominating naval warfare. Anti-submarine techniques evolved to counter the submarine threat but it was the post war period when really effective equipment became available.

The modern warship is awesome in comparison to its predecessors with miniature electronics and computer power used to link radar, sonar and other sensors with weapon systems. Using the data obtained, the target can be determined and missiles fired in seconds although this target may be well over the horizon - perhaps several hundred miles away.

The problem with this leap forward in technology has been the staggering increase in cost. Over the past few years, with most of the world suffering from several years of recession, the military has been hard hit by the politicians trying to save money.

Unfortunately for the military, it is perceived as fair game for budget cuts in peace-time recession.

While most of the UK Defence Reviews of recent years have resulted in continued reductions in Royal Navy strength, the 'Front Line First' Defence Costs Study of 1994 will result in a slight reversal of these trends if all the plans announced are completed.

Invitations to tender have been given by MoD for a further batch of seven Sandown MCMVs and three Batch 2 Trafalgar SSNs with an option for a further two although the four Upholder SSKs have been de-commissioned. Plans for further quantities of Type 23 frigates are remain on the books. In 1993 an order was placed for a new helicopter carrier (LPH) and it is hoped that an Invitation to Tender will be issued soon for the replacement of the assault ships HMS *Fearless* and *Intrepid*. Preliminary joint work continues with France on the New Generation Frigate to replace the Type 42 destroyers while feasibility studies for future afloat support requirements to enable replacement of the 'O' Class tankers.

On the aircraft front, 44 of the EH101 Merlins have been ordered to eventually replace the Sea King in the ASW role. The existing Lynx and Sea Harrier fleets are undergoing Mid Life Upgrades (MLUs) while that of the Sea King is almost complete. A further 18 Sea Harrier FA.2s have been ordered

The British nuclear deterrent comprises one nuclear-powered, ballistic missile armed submarine on patrol at any one time. To maintain this strength a fleet of four SSBNs are required. The Polaris submarines have maintained this capability for the past 25 years and the Trident armed Vanguard class

Below: The Sea Harrier FA.2 is already in service and 44 of the naval version of the Merlin helicopter have been ordered for the Royal Navy.

Opposite page: The impressive size of the *Vanguard* Class of submarine can only be seen when they are out of the water.

SSBNs are currently replacing them for the future.

In view of the ending of the Cold War, the apparent threat from the former Soviet and Warsaw Pact countries no longer exists. In theory therefore, the SSBNs are no longer required to provide this deterrent. However, most of the weaponry that provided the threat still exists but now under the control of a number of countries. We have already encountered a major conflict with Iraq and the Royal Navy is active in the attempts to restore peace to the former Yugoslavia along with a considerable force from the Army and Royal Air Force in addition to a number of other nations.

The SSBNs could be used for a wide number of roles in addition to the nuclear deterrent. The Trident missile is capable of carrying a range of payloads and some of these may be considered for the future. Depending on the nature of a future conflict, it is possible that a missile could be used to launch a surveillance and/or communications satellite over

the area of tension. Tactical nuclear or conventional warheads could be used should other means of delivery be inappropriate. Once the SSBN has been commissioned the massive capital cost has been expended. The operating costs are relatively inexpensive but to earn its keep its capabilities must be fully exploited.

MoD is examining the possibility of acquiring Tomahawks to arm the SSNs. With a range of 900km, the Tomahawk can be launched from the torpedo tubes and is an extremely capable weapon as was demonstrated by the American forces against Iraqi targets during the Gulf War.

While it would be a fine ideal to abandon the nuclear weapons it is considered in British circles that this would increase the possibility of a major conflict. This reasoning behind this is that the conventional warheads can be very accurate with today's technology but the threat of the nuclear weapon provides an ultimate threat due to the destructive force and environmental damage.

Although these is a moderated amount of good news Rosyth does not benefit and is to loose the minor war vessels of the Third Mine Counter Measures Squadron (MCM) and the Minewarfare element of the Small Ships Operation Training Staff (SSOTS) which will be moving to Faslane. The rest of the SSOTS together with the First MCM Squadron and the Fishery Protection Squadron are being deployed to Portsmouth.

RNAS Portland will also be a victim in that in 1999 it is intended to move the Lynx Squadrons to RNAS Yeovilton and close the Air Station down. With the operational sea training moving from Portland to Devonport in 1996 some 150 years of RN presence at Portland will cease.

In an attempt to reduce costs, contractorisation has been introduced to the grading and elementary flying training courses together with maintenance and servicing of many of the second-line units. Current MoD thinking envisages the formation of a Defence Helicopter Flying School to train aircrew of all three services. This would probably be located at AAC Middle Wallop or RAF Shawbury as RNAS Culdrose would be unable to accommodate a unit of this size.

The Army hospital at Aldershot and the RAF Princess Alexandra Hospital at Wroughton near Swindon are earmarked to close leaving the Royal Naval Hospital, Haslar in Gosport to meet the Services' future medical needs.

These equipment programmes would appear to be stabilising the past decline in Royal Navy strength but the manpower levels continue to be eroded. 'Front Line First' estimates 1,900 or 4.1 per cent reduction in RN manpower and a total of nearly 19,000 defence jobs in total. Contractorisation may have financial advantages for the Treasury but what will happen during the next conflict. For instance, should 899 Squadron be required to fulfil its front line role will the Hunting ground crew join the aircraft carriers bound for the war-zone to continue their work?

Despite the loss of the East-West confrontation, the world has become a less stable place with many emerging nations trying to establish their place in the new world order. The politicians see the end of the confrontation as providing a peace dividend and that they will now be able to save vast sums of money. The military can be likened to an insurance policy. You have to keep paying the premiums although you hope that you will not have to make a claim. You can reduce the premiums by taking out a cheaper policy but when you need to make a claim you find that you do not have the right cover.

By continually reducing the Defence Budget, each of the Services is gradually being strangled. However, the tasking is not being reduced, in fact in many cases it is being expanded. Prior to the Falklands War and the Gulf War defence cuts were being implemented and were only temporarily halted for the duration. On both occasions once the fighting was over the cuts continued. The current sit-uation in the former Yugoslavia continues to absorb a significant portion of Royal Navy capabilities supporting UN resolutions.

The role of the West Indies Guardship is carried out by various types of Royal Navy warships. They have various functions of which one is the working with other agencies to control to movement of drugs. In addition, due to the violent weather conditions, the ships are frequently requested to provide assistance to coastal villages or even whole islands that have been hit by hurricanes.

While it must train for its war role, the Royal Navy is frequently requested to assist in civil or humanitarian matters. The helicopters provide a rescue service to holiday makers in difficulty around out coast as well as for any ships in distress. Servicemen and women are called upon to assist in local disasters such as flooding or assisting police. The role in the former Yugoslavia is humanitarian while in Hong Kong the control of drugs and illegal immigrants is the priority role.

The Royal Navy is a valuable national asset in many ways apart from its fighting capability. The arrival of a Task Force can have a sobering effect on a aggressive country. If the desired effect is not achieved and the situation deteriorates the capability is there to assist in the evacuation of any nationals. A port visit by all or part of a Task Force can be seen as a gesture of friendship and support. The ability to provide assistance to anybody during a personal or national disaster will usually help to foster good relations for the future.

Left: Further RN operations support the UN in Cambodia.

Submarines

By comparison with the age-old tradition of the surface warship, the submarine is a relative newcomer to naval warfare. The Royal Navy's first such craft was a nine-man submarine built by Vickers Sons & Maxim that was launched on 2 October 1901 and named HM Submarine Torpedo Boat No. 1, *The Holland*. Although fearing that this form of warfare would eventually threaten its own surface fleet should it prove successful, the Admiralty was reluctant to develop submarines. However, five were eventually built.

In World Wars 1 and 2 the Germans led the world in submarine design and warfare. During World War 2 their U-boats sank a total of some 14 million tons of Allied merchant shipping. To a maritime nation like Britain this proved disastrous and much

'Vanguard' Class

Pennant No.	Ship
S05	*Vanguard*
S06	*Victorious*
S07	*Vigilant*
S08	*Vengeance*
Displacement	16,000 tonnes
Length	150.0m
Beam	19.5m
Speed	25kts submerged
Complement	132
Armament	Trident 2 SLBM, Spearfish and Tigerfish torpedoes, Sub-Harpoon SGM

Right: HMS *Vanguard*. In 1980 the British Government announced that it was to order the Trident I Submarine Launched Ballistic Missile (SLBM), based on the Trident C-4 missile. However, the US Department of Defense subsequently opted for the larger and more powerful Trident II system with the D-5 missile to be fitted to the US Navy (USN) 'Ohio' Class SSBNs.

The British order was changed for Trident II and as a result the SSBN design was altered from that based on the missile compartment of the USN '640' Class to that of the 'Ohio' Class. However, the Royal Navy's boats are to be fitted with 16 tubes compared with the USN's 24.

Above: HMS *Vanguard*. The Trident SSBNs are powered by a Pressurised Water Reactor (PWR2) that is also fitted to the British hunter-killer submarines. This reactor has a longer core life than the earlier PWR1, increasing time between refits. It also helps reduce its noise footprint, making it more difficult to detect.

effort was put into countering the threat posed by enemy submarines.

Today, the Royal Navy's submarines are formidable vessels. With the advent of nuclear power, boats of the Trident and Polaris classes can circumnavigate the globe carrying a massive nuclear deterrent without ever needing to surface. The modern diesel-electric Patrol submarine is a fast, silent and difficult boat to detect, armed with the latest weaponry like Tigerfish or Sub-Harpoon with which it can launch a deadly attack.

Today's Royal Navy submarine flotilla is currently (1994) made up of the 'bomber' – or correctly termed (SSBN) – comprising the three remaining Polaris boats, HMS *Revenge* having been paid off in April 1992. These will be replaced gradually by the Trident-equipped 'Vanguard' Class submarines, the first of which is now in service. The role of the nuclear-powered Fleet hunter/killer submarines (SSN) is to provide protection for British and Allied naval and merchant vessels, wherever a potential threat is perceived from enemy warships or submarines. Finally, there are the shorter-range diesel-electric Patrol submarines (SSK), although current defence plans are resulting in the 'Upholder' Class of SSKs being withdrawn. However, the improved 'Trafalgar' Class SSK is due to begin construction within the next few years.

Right: *Vanguard* is seen being eased carefully alongside at Faslane. At 16,000 tonnes *Vanguard* is over twice the displacement of the Polaris boats, although she is only 20 metres longer.

Right: The spacious control console of the 'Vanguard' Class submarines is in pleasant contrast to the cramped 'O' Class, the last boat of which was retired only in 1993.

Each boat has two crews of 132 – Port and Starboard – of which one is on patrol while the other is ashore training or on leave. They work in a spotless air-conditioned environment on four decks which also accommodate the work and rest compartments. Power is supplied by the PWR2 reactor, located aft of the missile tubes, which drives two turbines to produce 27,500shp. An auxiliary diesel generator is also fitted and produces 2MW.

Right: *Vanguard* is fitted with the 2054 Sonar system, unique to this class of submarine. It uses an array of hydroplanes and transducers twice the size of those currently used by the Royal Navy. The raw data from the array is fed into the Sonar Room computer where it is processed to provide the Commanding Officer with information on the range, bearing, speed and identity of any vessels detected.

Left: The SubMarine Command System (SMCS) is the 'brain' of the tactical weapon system aboard the Trident submarine. Data fed from the various sensors is assessed and presented to the Commanding Officer to keep him fully informed and able to make the necessary decisions. Once a decision has been made, the SMCS converts the commands into action commands that will prepare, provide guidance and launch the tactical weapons. The 'Vanguard' Class are also fitted with four 21in (533mm) torpedo tubes from which they can launch Spearfish and Tigerfish torpedoes, and Sub-Harpoon anti-ship missiles.

Left: The 'Vanguard' Class SSBN can carry 16 of the US-built Trident D-5 missiles and each can be fitted with up to 12 British-built warheads in a carrier or 'bus'. The Trident is a three-stage solid propellant missile measuring 13.42m long and weighing some 130,000kg. It has a range of over 6,500km. As part of the deterrent value of the SSBNs, the number of missiles and total number of warheads carried is classified. However, it has been announced that a maximum of 96 will be fitted.

A proposal is being considered for the fitting of tactical nuclear warheads to retain the credibility of the SSBN against a non-nuclear threat. This has come about with the ending of the Cold War and the reduction of the threat posed by forces of the USSR and the Warsaw Pact. In addition, Trident will also be used to replace the RAF's WE177 weapon in the nuclear sub-strategic deterrent role when it is retired from service.

'Resolution' Class

Pennant No.	Ship
S22	*Resolution*
S23	*Repulse*
S26	*Renown*
Displacement	7,000 tonnes
Length	129.5m
Beam	10.1m
Speed	20kts surfaced /25kts submerged
Complement	143 (x2)
Armament	Polaris A3 SLBM, Tigerfish torpedoes

Above: *Renown* is the third of the Polaris SSBNs. She was built by Cammell Laird at Birkenhead and commissioned in December 1968. Since 1969, at least one of these boats has provided a nuclear deterrent by remaining on operational readiness to fire its missiles should Britain ever be attacked. They will continue to do so in a diminished form until the final boat makes way for the fourth of the 'Vanguard' Class that will replace it.

Resolution was the first of the Polaris submarines to serve in the Royal Navy and put to sea operationally for the first time in July 1968. With her keel laid down at Vickers' Barrow shipyard during early 1964 this was quite an achievement for such a complex boat.

Below: Each boat is powered by the Rolls-Royce PWR1 that provides steam for the propulsion turbines and turbo-generators that produce over 11.2MW (15,000shp). The almost unlimited power provides all types of comfort for the crew: the air-conditioning removes carbon dioxide and dust while electrolysers extract oxygen from the water. Up to 5,000 gallons a day of fresh water is produced from either of the two distillation plants. *Renown* was the last Polaris boat to be refitted now that the 'Vanguard' Class is entering service.

Left: Aboard *Renown* the Planesmen seem more like the pilot and co-pilot of a bomber aircraft than a submarine. The complement of an SSBN is divided into a Port and Starboard crew, each consisting of 143 officers and ratings. One crew will be at sea while the second will be ashore, either on leave or training.

Living conditions aboard a 'bomber' are comparable with that in any modern surface warship. Accommodation is comfortable while the galley is able to provide several choices of hot and cold meals. A cinema equipped with a large stock of modern films is provided together with a large library. Facilities are also available for language and correspondence courses. A daily newspaper is published to keep the crew informed, while individual members of the crew can each receive a message from home. Unfortunately, these messages cannot be acknowledged because the transmissions would give away the location of the boat.

Left: In common with every other Royal Navy warship when alongside, armed Royal Marines maintain a guard on *Renown* to ensure any intruders are repelled. Today's threat is not so likely to come from Eastern Block infiltrators, but from the CND demonstrators who still try to make their waning presence felt. Following attacks on other military establishments, a real threat exists from terrorists and the Royal Marine Commachios are specially trained for this scenario.

Renown is pictured here alongside at Faslane; this is the only time that one is likely to see an operational SSBN, apart from when it is departing or returning to Faslane.

Right: To ensure that each missile is fully operational, various systems checks are regularly made. Here in the missile compartment of *Renown* the checklist is completed. The sealed door is an inspection porthole into the missile tube.

Lower right: The 'Resolution' Class of submarines has provided the British nuclear deterrent since 1969. Although declining in numbers, the class will continue to fulfil this role until it is finally handed over to the 'Vanguard' Class SSBNs. The US Navy withdrew its Polaris missiles in the mid-1970s.

Each 'Resolution' Class SSBN was originally built to accommodate 16 Polaris A-3 missiles. These were the US-built UGM-27C missile that was fitted with a British designed and built triple warhead of some 200 kilotons. These were later upgraded to maintain the effectiveness of the system. Code named 'Chevaline', the existing warhead was incorporated within a new manoeuvrable re-entry vehicle to which advanced penetration equipment had been incorporated. The missiles were subsequently redesignated A-3TK.

The Polaris is a two-stage solid propellant missile. It is 9.55m long and weighs 13,600kg and has a range of over 4,000km. This distance is significant because the furthest place from any sea is Lake Baikal in Central Asia – 2,750km from the nearest coast.

While on the surface a submarine is always vulnerable, but once it has dived it enters another world. Over the years there have been many advances in the understanding of the effects of temperature and salinity layers within the ocean depths. A submarine will now use these to great effect to conceal itself from the probing sensors of ships and aircraft. The SSBN must be able to hide effectively but, by using its sensors, must always be aware of any nearby ships or submarines that might pose a threat.

Encounters with fishing boats – and in particular their nets – have always presented a problem. In 1993 a trial attempt was made to resolve this problem by fitting acoustic 'pinger' sonars to the nets of fishing vessels based in the Clyde, to alert the submarines to their presence.

'Swiftsure' Class

Pennant No.	Ship
S104	*Sceptre*
S105	*Spartan*
S106	*Splendid*
S108	*Sovereign*
S109	*Superb*
Displacement	4,400 tonnes
Length	82.90m
Beam	10.1m
Speed	30+kts submerged
Complement	116
Armament	Tigerfish torpe-does, Sub-Har-poon SSM, mines

Left and below: *Swiftsure* was the first of this class of nuclear-powered Fleet submarines (SSN) to succeed the 'Valiant' Class of Fleet submarine. She was commissioned in 1973 but paid off in 1992. However, the rest of these SSNs continue in service and receive improvements to sensors and other vital equipment during refits to maintain their capabilities. Shown here is HMS *Sparton*. It is anticipated that the 'Swiftsure' Class will continue to provide valuable service well into the next century.

Right: Operators of the Fire Control use information from the various sensors to analyse the target. Defensive measures are prepared and the captain decides on the appropriate response to be made.

Right: An internal view of the Weapons Stowage Compartment of *Superb* showing a Sub-Harpoon at the top right and Tigerfish at the bottom right.

The Mk 24 Tigerfish is 6.5m long, weighs 1,551kg, has a maximum speed of 35kts and a range of up to 22kms. It was developed to meet the Royal Navy's requirement for a long-range advanced active and passive acoustic heavyweight homing torpedo, for anti-submarine or anti-ship engagement. Designed to be submarine-launched, Tigerfish is initially wire-guided but is fitted with its own homing device for the final attack. In service, the Tigerfish has proved to be an exceptionally quiet torpedo but it is planned to replace it with the Spearfish from the mid-1990s.

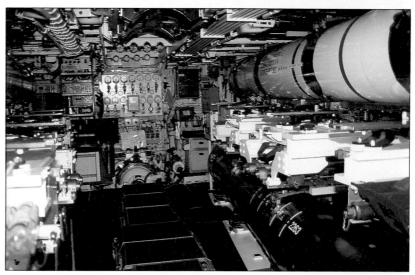

Right: Power for the 'Swiftsure' and 'Trafalgar' Class of attack submarines is provided by a Rolls-Royce PWR1 nuclear reactor. Producing some 11.2MW (15,000shp) the SSNs can remain operational for almost indefinite periods submerged. The condition of the reactor is constantly monitored by the reactor operators.

Left: Submarines are no exception when it comes to the provision of good food. Although the facilities may be a little cramped for a complement of 116, the numbers requiring feeding at any one time are not too much to handle.

Lower left: *Spartan* is seen here during a deperming trial at HMS *Neptune*'s Interim Deperming Facility (IDPF) at Faslane, designed for the magnetic treatment of the 'Vanguard' Class SSBNs.

All steel-hulled vessels acquire a magnetic signature that can be detected by aircraft, or the triggering mechanism in mines. For submarines to retain their covert capabilities this magnetic signature must be removed. This is achieved by subjecting the vessel to a controlled magnetic field.

IDPF requires the manual wrapping of the submarine with coils of electrical cable. These are used to generate the necessary magnetic force field that reduces the natural magnetic signature of the boat. Originally it had been intended to build an off-shore sail-in facility for the 'Vanguard' and other classes of submarines, but this was cancelled due to the rapidly escalating costs. In view of this and the changing requirements on the submarine flotilla, a relatively cheap alternative was designed, built and proved before *Vanguard* arrived. The IDPF has a design life of six years and, consequent on its effectiveness, ease and frequency of use, the viability of its successor system will depend.

'Trafalgar' Class

Pennant No.	Ship
S87	*Turbulent*
S88	*Tireless*
S90	*Torbay*
S91	*Trenchant*
S92	*Talent*
S93	*Triumph*
S107	*Trafalgar*
Displacement	4,700 tonnes
Length	85.4m
Beam	9.8m
Speed	32kts
Complement	130
Armament	Spearfish and Tigerfish torpedoes, Sub-Harpoon SSM, mines

Opposite page, bottom: The 'Trafalgar' Class fleet of SSNs is far advanced from the hunter-killers of World War 2. Manned by a crew of 130, these nuclear-powered submarines are crammed full of the very latest sonar and navigation equipment.

Visible over the hull of the submarine is a pattern of squares. The hull is actually covered by special rubber tiles which are fitted to all Royal Navy submarines to reduce the transmission of noise from within the submarine. These noises are produced by engine, machinery and equipment and can be detected by an enemy's passive sonar. The tiles also act to absorb sounds transmitted by an active sonar.

Top right: Once located and in position, the SSN has a deadly arsenal of torpedoes and Harpoon anti-shipping missiles to unleash.

Here a Spearfish torpedo is loaded into one of the 'Trafalgar' Class boats.

Right: The heavyweight Tigerfish and Spearfish torpedoes are displayed here alongside the smaller and lighter weight Sting Ray. Weighing 1,850kg, Spearfish is a heavyweight torpedo that measures approximately 6m long. Although wire-guided, Spearfish has an onboard computer which enables it to adjust its heading for the target despite any avoiding action – even the cutting of its wire link.

The sensors in the nose of Spearfish contain passive and active sonars, the first of which would normally be used during the initial attack, while the active sonar might be used in the final stages.

Spearfish is powered by a Sunstrand Type 21TP01 gas-turbine engine, rather than the conventional electric motor, which enables it to reach speeds of 75kts at ranges of up to 21km.

Left: The UGM-84B Sub-Harpoon missile is the submarine-launched variant of the AGM-84 air-to-surface and the RGM-84 surface-to-surface missile. It is launched while the submarine is still submerged. Once the targeting data has been programmed the missile, which is enclosed in a capsule, can be fired from the torpedo tube. On breaking the surface the capsule nose cap is blown off and the missile commences free flight. The Sub-Harpoon is equipped with its own sensors and computers to locate and home onto the target.

Below: Escorted by an RMAS tug for safety, *Torbay* passes Plymouth Ho. One cannot but wonder what Sir Francis Drake would have made of these boats.

Right: *Triumph* rendezvous with a US Navy SSN at the North Pole while a RAF Nimrod flies overhead.

The 'Trafalgar' Class SSN has a world-wide capability. In 1993 *Triumph* returned home after a seven-month deployment to the Indian Ocean. During this time she made a port visit to Abu Dhabi and became the first Royal Navy SSN to operate in the Gulf. Following the entry into service of the Iranian 'Kilo' Class submarines, *Triumph* brought home much useful information regarding their operating techniques in the difficult Gulf waters.

On completion of the deployment, *Triumph* returned home via the Suez Canal. During the whole of her time away she had been operating without any dedicated forward support, thus displaying the SSN's excellent ability to operate for long periods on unsupported world-wide deployments.

'Upholder' Class Submarines

Pennant No.	Ship
S40	*Upholder*
S41	*Unseen*
S42	*Ursula*
S43	*Unicorn*
Displacement	2,400 tonnes
Length	70.3m
Beam	7.6m
Speed	12kts surfaced/20kts submerged
Complement	44
Armament	Spearfish and Tigerfish torpedoes, Sub-Harpoon SSM, mines

Right: When ordered for the Royal Navy, the 'Upholder' Class represented the very latest in diesel-powered submarines. Designed primarily for Anti-Submarine Warfare (ASW) and Anti-Surface Vessel warfare (ASV), this class of submarine is also used for surveillance, intelligence gathering, mining and training. Unfortunately a problem with the weapon discharge system meant that the class was initially incapable of undertaking its primary role. The 'Upholder' submarines have since been modified to rectify this problem and the trials have been successfully completed.

The ending of the Cold War and the reduction of the perceived threat has led to a reduction in the requirement for this type of submarine. It can be argued that, following the withdrawal of the 'Oberon' Class, there is still a real place for the 'Upholder' submarines in the modern Royal Navy. Although they have been offered for lease or sale, it has not been discounted that they may be placed in storage for potential future Royal Navy service. A large amount of money has been spent building and bringing them up to a fully operational state and it would seem foolhardy to dispose of them while the world remains in such a turbulent state. One may find that in a few years' time circumstances may again require such a boat, but the cost inevitably will be much higher.

Left: Operators in the Fire Control Compartment monitor data received from the various sensors.

The '2400' Class, as they were originally known, were designed to incorporate the experience gained from the continued development of the UK nuclear and diesel-electric submarines. As a result the 'Upholder' Class has a far greater capability than previous boats in terms of combat, performance, stealth, resistance to attack and safety. It also has the potential for modification to ensure that the class will remain effective well into the future.

Above: The 'Upholder' Class SSK is fitted with the Ferranti DCC Tactical Data Handling System (TDHS) that provides the Action Information Organisation (AIO) and Fire Control System (FCS). This was derived from similar systems in previous Royal Navy nuclear submarines. The TDHS receives information from a variety of inputs ranging from sonar, arrays, radar and periscope for evaluation. This enables the system to calculate speed, range and bearing data that is presented on screen for command decision. Depending on the nature of the threat and the response input into TDHS by the operators, the weapons FCS will initiate the launch sequence of the appropriate weapons.

Right: The 'Upholders' are powered by a pair of supercharged 16-cylinder Paxman Valenta engines that provide the propulsive and battery-charging requirements. In order to store the electrical power the class is fitted with two 240 lead/acid cell batteries, sufficient to produce a submerged speed of over 20kts for short distances. It has a totally submerged range of over 250nm at 4kts and over 8,000nm when submerged but utilising its snort. It can dive to depths of over 200m.

Each 'Upholder' boat has an extremely powerful combat suite, situated in a control room on No. 1 deck which has no passageways in order to reduce operator distractions. The Combat and Control System (CCS) combines long-range passive sonar with medium-range active and passive (plus intercept) sonar, for which it has analysis, classification and passive ranging arrays. This information is then processed by a TDHS computer which produces weapon fire information to be fed directly to the weapons.

Below: There are 18 shock-protected weapon stowages in the weapon stowage compartment to accommodate the range of torpedoes, missiles or mines that would be fed to the six torpedo tubes. Not visible in this view are the submarine mines.

Aircraft Carriers

It was Lieutenant Samson who made the first launch of an aircraft from a ship in 1911 when he used a platform on the bows of the battleship HMS *Africa*. Many aircraft were deployed aboard ships during the early stages of World War 1; they were lowered over the side for take-off, landed back on the water and then recovered by crane. It was not until 2 August 1917 when Squadron Commander E. H. Dunning DSC, Royal Naval Air Service (RNAS), became the first man to land on a ship that the full potential of this technique began to be realised. Unfortunately Dunning was killed a few days later while repeating the feat with his Sopwith Pup aboard HMS *Furious*. Subsequently, this ship was fitted with a flush deck to become the first aircraft carrier.

During the inter-war years, naval aviation progressed slowly within the control of the RAF, and it was not until May 1939 that the Admiralty regained administrative control once more. Despite the strides that had been made, the old-fashioned attitude in the Admiralty considered that an enemy could only be effectively attacked when within the range of guns. As a result the development of dedicated carrier-borne aircraft had been neglected, and those then in use were obsolete. Although the Royal Navy had seven carriers at the outbreak of war, only *Ark Royal* could be considered modern. The Fleet Air Arm (FAA) was equally poorly equipped for the conflict that was looming.

It was on 11 November 1940 that 21 Fairey Swordfish biplane torpedo bombers took off from the new *Illustrious*. One had to turn back but the rest of the force flew 170 miles to the heavily defended Italian harbour at Taranto. Here the Swordfish attacked the Italian battle fleet that were at anchor. This action in which the Italian fleet was crippled by such a relatively small force was to have a major impact on the outcome of the war. From then on the FAA and aircraft carriers played an ever increasing role in naval operations and included attacks on many German warships, including the *Bismarck* and

Invincible' Class aircraft carriers

Pennant No.	Ship
R05	*Invincible*
R06	*Illustrious*
R07	*Ark Royal*

(Data for *Ark Royal* in brackets)

Displacement	20,000 tonnes (20,000 tonnes)
Length	206.00m (210.00m)
Beam	32.00m (36.00m)
Speed	28kts
Complement	666 + 366 air crews
Armament	Sea Dart missiles, 2 x 20mm GAM-BO1 guns, 3 x 30mm Goal keeper guns
Aircraft	8 x Sea Harrier, 12 x Sea King (9 x HAS.7, 3 x AEW.2)

Below: The primary task of the *'Invincible'* Class of aircraft carrier is to act as command ship for the anti-submarine force. The Royal Navy has three ships of this class, the first built was *Invincible* commissioned on 11 July 1980. Clearly visible here is the stern-mounted Goalkeeper Close-in Weapons System (CIWS).

Below: On 1 November 1985 the third and final ship of the class entered service, *Ark Royal*. The fleet of three carriers ensures that two ships can be operational and at sea, while the third can be in refit or reserve.

Tirpitz. Escort carriers were also being used to protect convoys against the U-boat threat.

Only a year after the end of World War 2, the first ever deck landing by a jet aircraft was made and in the following year the first landing was made by a helicopter on a naval vessel at sea. A world leader in technology, the FAA introduced the steam catapult, angled deck and the mirror landing sight. Later, to this was added the first landing of a Vertical Take-Off and Landing (VTOL) aircraft on a carrier. Along with these developments, the weight and capabilities of the aircraft increased through Sea Hawk and Scimitar to Buccaneer and Phantom.

The FAA suffered a setback when the fleet carriers were withdrawn, but they were soon to be replaced by a new class of ship – the Through Deck Cruiser. Designed to operate the revolutionary Vertical/Short Take-Off and Landing (V/STOL) Sea Harrier, this ship no longer needed the catapults, arrester wires or angle deck because this aircraft could take-off and land more like a helicopter. The last of the old carriers was *Hermes* which was converted to the anti-submarine role and later further adapted for amphibious warfare, being still able to operate Sea Harriers.

When the new Through Deck Cruisers were being built, a Royal Navy officer, Lieutenant-Commander Taylor, offered the theory that a Sea Harrier's performance could be greatly enhanced by using a ramp for take-off. The result was that the Sea Harrier could carry an extra 1,500lb of fuel or weapons. Following trials, all three 'Invincible' Class ships, as they were to become known, were modified. When the Falklands crisis broke in April 1982, *Invincible* and *Hermes* were deployed to the South Atlantic as part of the Task Force that sailed to regain the islands from the Argentinian invaders. The role of the aircraft carriers was invaluable as the nearest land point that could be used was Ascension Island, some 4,000 miles from the Falklands.

The current 'Invincible' Class of Royal Navy carrier is small by American standards. However, the vessels of the class are well suited for the Anti-Submarine Warfare (ASW) and amphibious warfare roles for which they were designed.

Below: The Westland Sea King is the only helicopter normally accommodated aboard the carriers, although the EH101 Merlin has been ordered eventually to replace it.

On the deck of *Ark Royal* can be seen the naval prototype Merlin while hovering alongside is the Sea King AEW.2, and at the rear the Sea King HC.4 used for Commando support.

The Merlin is fitted with the composite BERP blades that have an advanced aerodynamic tip. This gives the helicopter an extra 35 per cent lift for the same power setting compared with conventional blades.

Left: *Illustrious* was commissioned on 20 June 1982. She is seen here, still wrapped in scaffolding and weather protection during the final stages of her recent (1993) refit at Devonport. During this time *Illustrious* had her ski-ramp increased from 7 to 13 degrees and a 100-seat air crew briefing room added. The Phalanx was replaced by Goalkeeper and sponsons added for chaff and decoy systems. Accommodation and office space was increased and some mess decks were converted to cater for up to 100 female personnel.

Below: *Invincible* passes *Ark Royal* on departure from Portsmouth on another operational deployment.

Opposite page, bottom: *Ark Royal* under way. Aboard are eight Sea Harriers lined-up, plus some Sea Kings. Depending on the role, each aircraft carrier is equipped with nine Sea King HAS6 helicopters for the anti-submarine role. In addition, three Sea King AEW2s are operated to provide an Airborne Early Warning (AEW) capability for the force. Air defence and reconnaissance is the role of between six and eight Sea Harrier FRS.1s. The Sea Harrier is undergoing a Mid Life Update (MLU) and completed aircraft are designated FA.2. As sufficient aircraft become available each squadron will convert. An additional role of the carriers is to provide a helicopter platform for amphibious operations, for which some Sea King HC.4s may be accommodated. A maximum of 22 aircraft can be carried.

Right: Families and friends wave farewell from the Round Tower at the mouth of Portsmouth harbour as *Ark Royal* edges out into the Solent. Behind the Sea Harrier FRS.1s of 801 Squadron are members of the ship's company who are at Procedure Alpha.

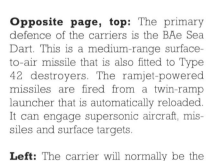

Opposite page, top: The primary defence of the carriers is the BAe Sea Dart. This is a medium-range surface-to-air missile that is also fitted to Type 42 destroyers. The ramjet-powered missiles are fired from a twin-ramp launcher that is automatically reloaded. It can engage supersonic aircraft, missiles and surface targets.

Left: The carrier will normally be the Flag Ship of a Task Force or Task Group. In this Task Group, the nearest ship is the USS *Kirk*, a 'Knox' Class frigate. Behind is the support tanker RFA *Brambleleaf* whose task it is to replenish the warships at sea. Next to her is *Invincible* while beyond is *Edinburgh*, a 'Sheffield' Class Type 42 Batch 3 guided-missile destroyer. She supplies air defence for the Group, while also providing anti-ship and shore bombardment and ASW capabilities.

Above: The General Dynamics Phalanx is a six-barrelled 20mm Close-In Weapon System (CIWS) that fires 6,000 rounds/min. It is designed to provide defence against anti-ship missiles. Following the Exocet experience of the Falklands War, Phalanx was fitted to meet the immediate operational needs in 1982. Here anti-missile defence proved to be a weakness and the CIWS is now considered a vital component of the short-range defence of a ship. At the time, Phalanx was the only operational system available and was easy to install, only requiring bolting to a suitably reinforced upper deck.

Left: The Signaal 30mm Goalkeeper anti-missile CIWS is being fitted to each 'Invincible' Class aircraft carrier during refits to replace the previously fitted Phalanx.

Goalkeeper uses the General Electric seven-barrelled GAU-8 gun that fires 4,200 rounds/min. The Goalkeeper system also incorporates a sophisticated radar that can track and search simultaneously. Most of the system is located below deck to enable an easier and safer working environment, but this makes it more difficult to install. As a result Goalkeeper will only replace Phalanx on the aircraft carriers, but it is also be installed on the four Type 22 Batch 3 frigates.

Three sets of Goalkeeper are being fitted to each carrier to provide a complete 360-degree coverage. When activated each gun operates autonomously. Using its own radar the target is tracked and the threat assessed. If the target is hostile, its heading is calculated by the Goalkeeper's own computer and then fired upon.

Left: The BMARC/Oerlikon 20mm GAM-B01 Naval Gun is fitted to several Royal Navy vessels. It is designed for use in both surface or anti-aircraft roles and fires at a rate of 1,000 rounds/min.

The GAM-B01 is a simple but reliable gun requiring no power, the gun being laid by the gunner using a shoulder harness.

Right: The Ops Room is the nerve centre of a modern warship. It is from here that overall command of the ship's weapons and equipment is exercised. Information is provided by radar, sonar and other sensors, plus communications from other ships. It is fed into the ship's computer to present an up-to-the-minute tactical picture of what is going on in the air, on the surface and under the waves to Command level. This enables the reaction time to any potential threat to be reduced to a minimum.

Above: Still very much a part of the modern Royal Navy is the signalling lamp. The passing of messages from one ship in a Task Force to another by Morse code ensures that the enemy is unable to monitor communications. Its main drawback is its lack of range in very poor weather conditions.

Left: The various elements of the Ops Room of *Invincible* are linked to a computer system through the Ferranti/Plessey ADAWS 6 (Action Data Automation Weapon System). The same system has been installed in *Illustrious*, but a slightly different system is used on *Ark Royal*, designated ADAWS 10.

The Action Information Organisation (AIO) is extremely powerful. It is required to provide information not only for its own weapons, but also to the aircraft and helicopters plus the command and control of other vessels of the Task Force.

Below: During 'Action Stations' all the crew are required to wear anti-flash clothing comprising of headgear and gloves. This is to reduce the effect on personnel of a shell or missile hitting the ship, and the resulting flash-fire causing serious burns to the exposed parts of the body.

On the bridge the Officer of the Watch takes bearing on other vessels to ensure that there is no likelihood of collision between vessels.

Right: Down below tension mounts in Damage Control, where the crew await damage reports following any attack on the ship – simulated or otherwise.

Below left: On one wall a detailed plan of the ship's structure enables rapid assessment of damage location, confinement and repair where necessary.

Below right: Teams assemble at designated positions throughout the ship, don protective clothing, and await instructions to go to the damaged area.

A major problem aboard a ship is fire because the smoke can spread rapidly and incapacitate the crew extremely quickly. Fire crews are equipped with the Thermal Imaging Camera (TIC) that enables the user to see through smoke to detect injured members of the ship's company.

Right: Non-essential combat crews have a secondary training in first aid. Casualties are brought to a central location where their injuries are assessed and treated. In a conflict, the most severely injured probably would be airlifted to a Primary Casualty Receiving Ship for intensive care and stabilising.

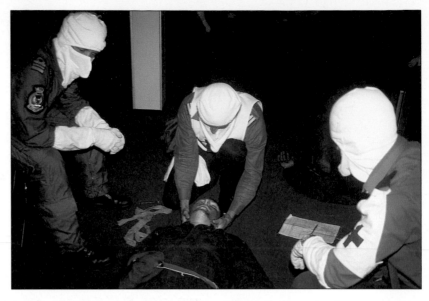

Below: In the Ship Control Centre the Engineering Officer and his team ensure that the ship has sufficient power for the tasks it is required to undertake. Here, speed instructions from the bridge are interpreted and the appropriate combination of engines is used.

The ship's power is supplied by four Rolls-Royce Olympus gas turbines. These are the maritime version of the engine that powers the supersonic airliner Concorde. Any permutation of these immensely powerful engines can be coupled through a large gearbox to provide speeds of 28kts.

Electrical power is provided by eight Paxman Valenta diesel generators with enough capacity to light a modest sized town. The ship's main switch-board, which is also located in the Control Centre, ensures that electrical power is maintained to the vital areas of the ship. This includes a distillation plant that produces some 75,000 gallons of fresh water daily.

Right: Each carrier has a secondary role of amphibious warfare for which some Sea King HC.4s would be embarked. Other marks of Sea King could be used to transport troops if required, but would be unable to move large numbers quickly.

Opposite page, top: *Invincible* leads two Type 42 destroyers and a Type 22 Batch 3 frigate. By operating together as a Task Force each ship can play its primary function to the full, therefore providing a more powerful team.

Opposite page, bottom: As the first Sea King HC.4 lands, the primary task is to lash the helicopter down to ensure that it does not move when the ship rolls.

When involved in multi-helicopter operations space onboard becomes tight. It is the efficient deck handling that ensures all is conducted smoothly and safely.

Above: To reduce the amount of space helicopters take up on the flight deck, the main rotors and tail can be folded. The light grey Sea Kings are HAS.6s for ASW and are known as 'pingers', referring to the sonar equipment they carry. The dark green Sea King HC.4 is often referred to as a 'jungly'. This is due to its support of the Royal Marines on land.

Opposite page top: This Sea King AEW.2 of 849 Squadron has its rotors and tail folded and radar housing stowed. It is being brought up from the hangar deck below on one of two lifts. The radar housing remains in the stowed position until the Sea King is airborne.

Above: A carrier is fully operational 24 hours a day. With chains still lashing the Sea Harriers down, the aircraft are prepared for an early start.

Left: Aircraft prepared and ready for action. The ground crews ensure that the aircraft are ready for their task as the pilot walks out to the aircraft, having been fully briefed as to his sortie.

Depending on its task, each carrier is also usually equipped with six to eight Sea Harriers. These will primarily be used mainly for flying Combat Air Patrols (CAP) to provide the Task Force/Group with fighter protection. For this they would be fitted with Sidewinder air-to-air missiles. Alternatively, the aircraft might be used in the anti-ship role with the Sea Eagle missile. The Sea Harrier is fitted with the 30mm Aden cannon and can carry bombs or rockets for ground-attack.

Above: The Harrier/Sea Harrier family of aircraft owes its unique V/STOL capability to the Rolls-Royce Pegasus vectored thrust engine. The engine follows the same principle of a conventional turbofan engine but, in the case of the Pegasus, pressurised cold air is bled from the engine and exits through the forward nozzles. The hot air exits through the rear pair of nozzles. The lift and forward thrust is provided by rotating the jet nozzles from the vertical to the horizontal. Braking is achieved by vectoring the nozzles slightly forward. The air brake itself can only function when the aircraft is travelling at a reasonable speed in forward flight.

Directional control of any aircraft is achieved by moving the control surfaces in an air current, but with the Harrier in the hover there is little or no air current. To maintain directional control an additional quantity of compressed air is bled off the engine and vented out of small controllable vents in the nose, tail and wing tips.

Opposite page, top: The Sea Harrier can carry a variety of weapons. Here this aircraft is fitted with a Sea Eagle drill round under the wing for the ASV role, plus a pair of AIM-9L Sidewinder air-to-air missiles.

The Sidewinder is a US Navy-designed missile with its origins dating back to the early 1950s. It has been built in large numbers and over subsequent decades its development has resulted in it becoming the most popular and effective of current generation Western AAMs.

The BAe Sea Eagle is an anti-ship missile. Launched from the Sea Harrier, this sea-skimming weapon is powered by a small turbojet that gives it a 110km range. Its computer control enables an over-the-horizon attack profile and, if required, an ability to single out a specific ship type from a convoy.

Opposite page, bottom: To maintain a Sea Harrier pilot's skill in the art of hitting a moving target, the aircraft is fitted with a 75kg practice bomb. This bomb has an identical performance to a larger high explosive bomb, but is designed to give just a flash when it hits the water.

Above: In common with most modern combat aircraft, the Sea Harrier is fitted with a Head-Up Display (HUD). This is a piece of glass located in front of the pilot, above the instrument panel at the base of the windscreen, and on which the basic information for him to fly the aircraft is projected. This reduces his need to keep looking down at the cockpit instruments, and possibly interfering with his concentration.

Below: Under the watchful eye of the FlyCo, a Sea Harrier has lined up and is about to be launched. The Sea Harrier FRS.1 is fitted with the Blue Fox lightweight high-performance radar, designed for the role of a fighter and maritime strike aircraft. During the upgrade to FA.2 this radar will be replaced with Blue Vixen.

Above: For taking off from the ski-ramp, the Sea Harrier's engine nozzles face fully aft. On releasing the brakes the pilot accelerates the aircraft along the flight deck. As the aircraft climbs the ski-ramp he rotates the nozzles partially down to provide some lift while the aircraft continues to accelerate.

Below: To the pilot, the impression is like hitting a hump back bridge at speed. To the aircraft the effect is dramatic to the extent that 1,500kg of additional payload can be carried by the Sea Harrier. This can be utilised both to carry fuel to give extra range or provide additional weaponry. In practice this will usually be a combination of the two.

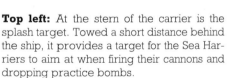

Top left: At the stern of the carrier is the splash target. Towed a short distance behind the ship, it provides a target for the Sea Harriers to aim at when firing their cannons and dropping practice bombs.

A burst of cannon fire from a Sea Harrier can be seen hitting the splash target while a pilot sits in his cockpit awaiting instructions to taxi out for take-off.

Left: A Sea King releases a Sting Ray light torpedo. This weapon is considered to be the most advanced lightweight anti-submarine torpedo currently in operational service throughout the world. Produced by GEC-Marconi, it is compatible with many platforms and can be launched from ships, fixed-wing aircraft and helicopters. It is fast, manoeuvrable and has a deep-diving capability and an ability to operate in shallow water. At the time of writing, over 2,000 Sting

Ray torpedoes have been ordered for the Royal Navy.

Top: The Depth Charge Mk. 11 (Mod. 3) is the latest variant of this family of weapons. It has been specially designed to withstand the rigours of helicopter operations, including the vibrations and the impact when hitting the sea. It can be fitted to various helicopters and aircraft but is seen here about to be fitted to a Sea King HAS.6.

The tail is designed to break off on impact with the water and thus provides part of the arming sequence of the depth charge.

Above: To ensure that the waters are safe from submarine attack, the Sea King will fly out to its designated area, probably well ahead of the Task Force. Here it will come into the hover and lower the Type 195M dipping sonar.

Above left: The acoustic returns from the dipped sonar or dropped sonar buoys are processed by the AQS 902 and presented on the MEL Sea Searcher display for the operator to analyse. This system can also plot radar returns and navigation data. However, the sonar is only as good as its operator so the returns will require interpreting. The sea has varying layers of water temperature and concentrations of salinity, which can provide various effects to deflect or distort the returns. This search will be repeated in a pattern all over the search area.

Left: While nuclear submarines (SSN and SSBNs) have sufficient reserves of power to circumnavigate the world without surfacing, diesel submarines (SSK) do not have the same advantage. While using electric motors for power when submerged, every SSK submarine must run its diesel generators to top up the power of its batteries. Operationally this would be accomplished while the submarine lies just below the surface using its snorkel. A submarine would only surface when its captain felt that a potential enemy was nowhere near.

Above: This Russian-built 'Kilo' Class diesel-powered submarine was not happy to have its picture taken. It was on delivery to the Iranian Navy and completed the whole voyage on the surface. With the introduction of this submarine into the Iranian Navy, this Middle Eastern country became the 43rd nation to operate submarines.

Below: Both *Invincible* and *Ark Royal* have spent considerable time in and around the Adriatic as part of the multi-national force in the former Yugoslavia. Their task has been to monitor and enforce UN Resolutions 816 and 836 in Operation 'Deny Flight'. Besides this task some combat aircraft, including the Royal Navy Sea Harriers, have been flying over Bosnia-Herzegovina fitted with bombs in case the commanders on the ground decide that air support is required.

Left: At the end of every sortie the Sea Harriers return to the carrier where they decelerate into a hover and it is at this time that the carrier is at its most vulnerable. The aircraft will be returning with low fuel and unable to hold off, so to assist them with their landing the ship must sail into the wind. For an ambushing submarine captain this can be a ideal opportunity. By carefully estimating the course of the carrier it is possible for him to remain submerged and lie still and not be detected by passive sonar. If his judgement is correct a successful torpedo attack could be mounted.

Consequently the ships and ASW Sea Kings have a mixture of active and passive sonars – the active giving the 'ping' while the passive only listens. The drawback of the active sonar is that its very action alerts the submarine crew that they are being searched for and that there is a possible target for them in the area. A defensive action for the Task Force is a constant alteration to its course, making it a very 'cat and mouse' operation.

Left: While on final approach the pilots are given hand directions from the flight deck to guide them onto a landing spot.

There is no need for elaborate deck systems such as steam catapults or arrester wires with the Sea Harrier, and therefore less deck area is required to operate these aircraft. Once on the deck, they are marshalled forward to make space for other aircraft to land.

Above: The harsh environmental conditions in which navy aircraft operate results in deposits of salt over most components, causing rapid corrosion. To minimise these problems, the aircraft are frequently coated in a light oil, but engines pose another problem. Once they have landed and taxi to their shut down point, demineralised water is sprayed into each of the Harrier's engine air intakes to flush out the salt.

Below: A Sea King HAS.6 of 814 Squadron returns to *Invincible* after an ASW sortie that may have lasted up to several hours and taken the helicopter way out beyond the horizon. Number two to land is a Sea King HC.4 from the RFA supply ship.

Above: Next to land is a Sea King AEW.2 from A Flight of 849 Squadron. This mark of Sea King is fitted with a modified version of the Searchwater long-range maritime surveillance radar as fitted to the RAF Nimrod. The adapting of Searchwater to fit into the Sea King was instigated following the destruction of HMS *Sheffield* and MV *Atlantic Conveyor* in the South Atlantic during the Falklands War.

Following the scrapping of the conventional carriers the Royal Navy lost its own Airborne Early Warning (AEW) aircraft, the Fairey Gannet. With the reduction of Britain's overseas commitments this was not thought to be a problem as an RAF land-based AEW aircraft would be available to provide cover. The Falklands was 2,000 miles from the nearest safe airfield and thus AEW cover was not available when it was needed.

One flight of three Sea King AEW.2s is always embarked on each carrier during any deployment. Included in its AEW function, this variant of the Sea King can also provide fighter direction and surface surveillance (for which this radar was originally developed). It also gives Over The Horizon Targeting (OTHT) for helicopter, surface or sub-surface launched missiles or the probe/strike control of friendly forces.

Below: With flying finished for the day it is the turn of the Sea King to be cleaned ready for the next day's flying.

Right: The rotor head of the Sea King is highly complex. It has to fulfil several functions of which the main one is the transmission of power from the engines to the blades. In flight it supports the helicopter using the lift generated by the blades. During this time it must endure the stress of constantly changing the pitch of the blade to provide directional control and lift. At the end of the day, when flying has finished, it must be able to fold the blades to reduce the deck space required by the helicopter.

On completion of flying, various checks are made to the helicopter and minor snags rectified. Pitot tubes are covered, as are engine intakes, to ensure no debris finds its way into sensitive instruments or the engine.

Below: When no longer required the Sea Harriers and Sea Kings will be returned to the hangar where it is environmentally more protective for the aircraft.

Top: In the hangar, there is an art to parking the aircraft to make them all fit in; but some careful thought is also required to ensure that the first aircraft that will be needed the next day is not the one parked down at the back.

Below: The normal ship's complement of aircraft is up to 8 Sea Harriers, 9 Sea King HAS.6s and 3 Sea King AEW.2s. When operating in the amphibious role the mix can be adjusted to accommodate a quantity of the Sea King HC.4. A maximum of 22 aircraft and helicopters can be accommodated. In order for the aircraft to remain fully operational, a comprehensive capability of servicing and maintenance is available. Here the wing has been removed and a replacement engine is being fitted to a Sea Harrier.

Above: Although a large amount of fuel and stores are kept on board, the aircraft carrier will require regular Replenishment At Sea (RAS) to maintain its fuel and stores reserves.

Here the RFA *Fort Austin* has moved abeam *Invincible* in readiness to commence a RAS.

Right: Once the ships are in position it is the job of the Gunline Party to fire a light line across to the other ship. This is then used to draw across the heavier ropes that will be used for the RAS.

Left: During a liquid RAS a group of pipes link the two ships through which fuel flows for the aircraft and the carrier, or diesel for the generators. Even fresh water can be provided.

Left: The final stage of stowing the stores is labour-intensive and requires as many of the crew as possible. They form a chain and shift the pallets of food, drink, equipment and other stores into their correct location.

Left: Some stores are obviously more valuable than others. Nevertheless, when shifting a quantity of stores in warmer climates it can get rather warm below deck.

Right: Bread is a major requirement at most mealtimes and is baked daily. The quantities of ingredients used on board ship even make Mrs Beeton's recipes look small.

Below: Soups are prepared in cauldrons...

Below right: ...and this recipe for sweet and sour only requires a couple of pints of vinegar!

Above left: After the meal a little light music! The visiting Royal Marines band rehearses between concerts for the ship's company. Trained at Deal in Kent, the musicians visit and provide entertainment on most ships and establishments. In addition they are frequently seen on ceremonial duties and are in great demand for public concerts. In time of war they would provide basic medical assistance.

Above: Not all rest days are so quiet and peaceful! With fitness a top priority in all the services, sport always appears high on the agenda. The deck of a carrier is an ideal place for a sports day.

Left: With most of the ship's company stood down, many take advantage of a little sun and fresh air while the Task Force transits the Suez Canal.

Left: Service personnel are frequently venting their energies to the benefit of a charity or good cause during their spare time. When the Orient '92 Task Force returned home, somewhere in the region of £10,000 had been raised.

One venture involved 146 members of the crew of *Invincible* spending half-hour shifts on a rowing machine. The rowing marathon commenced at Penang and was kept going for nine days non-stop until the ship arrived at Abu Dhabi – the distance clocked up was 4,194,348 metres.

Amphibious Warfare

The dedicated Amphibious Warfare (AW) ships are the Logistic Platform – Dock (LPD), known better as HMS *Fearless* and *Intrepid*. The first to enter service with the Royal Navy was *Fearless* in 1965 followed by *Intrepid* in 1967; both ships have been threatened with retirement for some time. In 1981 it was announced that both LPDs would be withdrawn but this decision was reversed following the vital role that they played in the Falklands War. *Intrepid* was paid off in 1991 and is currently in reserve at Portsmouth.

Designed specifically for amphibious operations, these ships can operate independently or as part of a Naval Assault Group. They can house a Brigade Headquarters when fitted with an Assault Operations Room. The LPDs can accommodate some 400 troops besides their crew of around 600, although space can be made for up to 1,000 troops.

The aircraft carriers can provide a useful extension for the amphibious force, but at the price of a reduced ASW and fighter capability. In May 1993 an order was placed for a Helicopter Carrier (LPH) that will be of similar size to the aircraft carriers.

Further extension to the amphibious force is provided by the Landing Ship – Logistic (LSL) fleet that is operated by the Royal Fleet Auxiliary (RFA). Meanwhile, Project Definition studies continue for the replacement of the LPDs.

Logistic Platform – Dock (LPD)

Pennant No.	Ship
L10	*Fearless*
L11	*Intrepid*
Displacement	11,582 tonnes
Length	158.0m
Beam	24.4m
Speed	20kts
Armament	2 x Sea Cat missile systems, 2 x 20mm Phalanx, 2 x 20mm GAM-BO1 guns, 4 x 30mm GCM-AO3 guns
Complement	635 + embarked force of up to 700

Left: With Royal Marine Gazelle helicopters on the flight deck and the dock flooded, *Fearless* takes part in another exercise.

These ships have an internal flooding capability to provide a dock for four LCUs that can each transport an MBT or up to 70 tons of vehicles or stores. In addition, they are equipped with four of the smaller LCVPs. These craft can transport a load of four tons.

Above: The Sea King HC.4 is the assault variant of this helicopter with Royal Marine Commando operations specifically in mind. It can carrying up to 27 fully armed troops or a range of underslung loads. The versatile Sea King is a vital part of the Marines' inventory.

Below: *Fearless* is fitted with two Phalanx and the GWS-20 Sea Cat missile system. The Short Sea Cat is a close-range surface-to-air missile designed for anti-aircraft defence, although it can be used against low-level missiles or surface targets within visual range. It has a radius of action of approximately 5,500m and is fitted with a proximity and contact fuse.

Right: *Fearless*'s Operations Room is equipped with the GEC-Marconi NAUTIS-L. This system provides all the command, control and navigation facilities for amphibious warships such as the LPDs. It utilises data from radar and other ship's sensors to provide facilities for the Task Force Commander. With this information at his fingertips he will be able to make effective decisions on all phases of amphibious warfare. This includes surveillance, target tracking, recovery of helicopters and landing craft, and self-defence, besides tactical and passage navigation.

Right: Below deck in the Assault Operations Room details of an emergency are beginning to emerge... an island has been hit by a hurricane... some of those stranded ashore are British Nationals. *Fearless* is the nearest ship! Sketchy details are pieced together and a plan is quickly put into action.

Right: Radio contact is made with groups ashore, establishing the locations of those requiring the most urgent help.

Left: With the initial party ashore a line of communication can be established and firsthand information reported to the ship.

Left: The Sea King provides the urgent airlift capability. With troops in the cabin, the urgently needed stores are placed in a net and flown as an underslung load.

Right: Following a breakdown of law and order, the initial party ashore has encountered several gangs of armed thugs who are taking advantage of the situation and are looting the wrecked buildings. Armed Royal Marines are posted to ensure the security of the landing zones and of the rescue parties.

Right: While some teams concentrate on preventing the spread of fires...

Right: ...others locate casualties and more survivors.

Right: Gathered at suitable locations, their identities are established and the wounds of the injured are assessed and prioritised by their degree of severity, while first aid is given. Transport is then arranged to the ship by helicopter or on a landing craft using the large dock facility.

Right: Once aboard, the large number of casualties will be tended to and treated by the ship's medics and doctors.

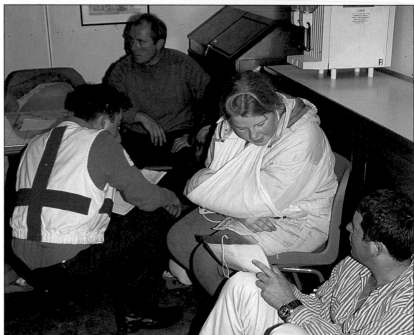

Right: Fortunately this event was what is referred to as a DISaSTer EXercise (DISTEX), a regular feature on the training programme of each Royal Navy ship. The Royal Navy has frequently been on the spot to render assistance to a range of civil emergencies.

For the exercise most civilians are played by servicemen, but they are often joined by families or local students and all parties benefit from the involvement.

Destroyers

The role of the destroyer is to provide defence of the Task Force/Group against air attack. This would be achieved through a layered defence of which the first layer is by directing Sea Harriers or RAF Tornados against the enemy attack while still at some distance. The second layer, for those enemy aircraft that have penetrated through the first, would be the ships' Sea Dart surface-to-air missile. For the closer range defence the Phalanx would be used. For ASW the Lynx would be used with its Sea Skua while the Sea Dart could be used for closer range.

Type 42 Batch 1 Destroyers

Pennant No.	Ship
D86	*Birmingham*
D87	*Newcastle*
D88	*Glasgow*
D108	*Cardiff*
Displacement	4,000 tonnes
Length	125.0m
Beam	14.6m
Speed	29kts
Complement	280
Armament	1 x twin Sea Dart system, 1 x 4.5in (114mm gun), 2 x 20mm Phalanx CIWS, Mk 44 or Stingray torpedoes, 2 x Oerlikon 20mm Mk.7 and/or 2 or 4 20mm GAM-BO1 guns
Aircraft	1 x Lynx helicopter

Right: The role of the destroyer is to provide area air defence for the Task Force/Group as well as shore bombardment. In addition the carrying of a helicopter provides an anti-submarine and anti-surface vessel capability.

The Royal Navy operates a total of 12 Type 42 destroyers which form the backbone of the Fleet's anti-air warfare force. They are also capable of dealing effectively with surface and submarine targets.

Left: The air defence capability is centred around the Sea Dart guided missile system which provides an area defence for the Task Force. It also has an effective capability against surface ships.

Left: Type 42s have a range of about 4,000 miles at 18kts. They are capable of 29kts but this would greatly reduce their range. RAS gives the ships an almost unrestricted range.

Above: As with most frigates and destroyers, the Type 42 has its own flight deck from which it operates the Lynx HAS.3. Visible on the flight deck of *Cardiff* is a thin black cable. When the Lynx is on the deck, this cable is plugged into the helicopter to allow secure communications between the air crew and the ship. This will allow information to be passed to the air crew up the last minute without alerting an eavesdropping enemy. As the Lynx takes off the cable automatically unplugs.

Also visible is a circular grill in the centre of the flight deck. In bad weather when the ship is rolling severely, the pilot may find it difficult to land the Lynx. With little option but to make the landing, a harpoon-like spike is lowered from the hovering helicopter. The spike passes through the grill and attaches itself. The pilot of the Lynx will maintain a climb setting on his flying controls while a winch will gradually wind the helicopter safely down to the deck.

Above: The Lynx proved itself during both the Falklands and the Gulf Wars. Lifting off from *Ark Royal*, this Lynx HAS.3 from *Cardiff* has kill markings painted on it to represent the number of Iraqi warships that it destroyed, mainly with Sea Skua.

A total of 10 Lynx HAS.3 were deployed to the Gulf aboard various ships. It was a Lynx from *Cardiff* that first fired in anger on 29 January 1991 when it launched a Sea Skua and destroyed an Iraqi landing craft. Within three days the Lynx from *Cardiff* and *Gloucester* had destroyed six more vessels. By the end of the conflict a total of 26 missiles had been fired and 15 Iraqi warships destroyed, some as the result of multiple missile firings.

Left: Same flight, another occasion! The Lynx HAS.3 is fitted with the Ferranti Seaspray radar that is optimised for the tracking of maritime vessels and aircraft. It can detect the periscope of submerged submarines as well the small high speed vessels capable of launching a missile attack. It also provides the tracking and guidance for the Sea Skua missile.

All operational Lynx belong to 815 Squadron that has its headquarters at RNAS Portland.

Right: The Type 42 is powered by two Rolls-Royce Olympus TM3B marine gas-turbines that each develop 25,000shp, plus two Rolls-Royce Tyne RM1C gas-turbines. The level of power required determines the configuration of engines used. For economical cruising the RM1Cs are used while acceleration to the top speed of 29kts would require the TM3Bs. Power from these engines is used to drive a pair of controllable pitch propellers.

The large wake made by the ship when it is sailing at near maximum speed certainly gives a great impression of the power from these engines.

Below: Seen here above the bridge is one of a pair of dome-mounted Type 909 Radars. This is the Sea Dart fire control radar. On either side of this are a pair of Marconi SCOT SATCOM antennae for communication including Marisat.

Below: Clearly visible here is the forward deck layout with the Vickers 4.5in Mk 8 gun located in front of the Sea Dart launcher

Left: The Type 42s are fitted with either the Type 2050 or Type 2016 Sonar. This provides data into the ADAWS that will provide aiming data to the Lynx for an attack on the submarine with air-launched torpedoes.

Fire control of the ship's other weapon systems, including the 4.5in gun and Sea Dart missiles, is conducted through the ADAWS that calculates and provides the necessary aiming computations.

The Ops Room of the Type 42s are fitted with the Ferranti ADAWS (Action Data Automatic Weapon System) to process the large amount of information provided by all the ship's sensors. The first batch have the ADAWS 4 while the Batch 2 and 3 have the ADAWS 7 and 8. Together with data from other ships in the Task Force, ADAWs is used to provide an over view and detail for the command in addition to advising threat levels.

Left: Using binoculars and assisted by TV, thermal imagers and laser range finders, the operator of the Director Aiming Sight is able to provide information to the fire control system, gun or missile mounts.

Left: The Fleet Target Group is frequently deployed aboard ship to fly the radio-controlled MATS-B to provide a training target for the ship's machine gunners.

For anti-aircraft missile training a 12ft-long jet-propelled target capable of Mach 0.8 is used.

Above: The 4.5in Mk 8 gun is fired during a (Principal Weapons Officer) PWO(A) course in the Mediterranean. With a single barrel, the Mk 8 is a lighter and more accurate design than the twin barrelled Mk 6 that it replaced. It is able to fire 25 rounds, each weighing 21kg, onto a target in one minute.

Right: Widely fitted on RN and RFA vessels, the BMARC/Oerlikon 20mm is a basic and simple light anti-aircraft gun that originates from World War 2. It has a rate of fire of 450 rounds/min and ammunition is fed from 58–round magazines.

Above: Even at speed the Type 42s have an impressive rate of turn.

Below: In the event of an injury aboard ship, all vessels have a Medical Officer and a treatment facility. It is possible that this may be insufficient for some accidents and require the patient to be transferred to a larger ship with the appropriate facilities. In the event of a helicopter being unavailable, the patient would be placed in a special stretcher and transferred by jackstay.

Right: *Newcastle* makes a turn to starboard giving the ship a distinct list. Clearly visible are her two Phalanx CIWS guns with their white radar domes. The large dome above the hangar is the Marconi Type 909 fire control radar. The pair of domes fore and above the Phalanx are the Marconi SCOT SATCOMs providing secure communications.

Above: All Type 42s are powered by COmbined Gas Or Gas (COGOG) configuration. The Batch 1 and 2 destroyers have a maximum speed of 29kts and a range of 4,000 miles at 18kts.

Type 42 Batch 2 Destroyer

Pennant No.	Ship
D89	*Exeter*
D90	*Southampton*
D91	*Nottingham*
D92	*Liverpool*
Displacement	4,000 tonnes
Length	125.0m
Beam	14.6m
Speed	28kts
Complement	280
Armament	(see Batch 1)
Aircraft	1 x Lynx helicopter

Below: The Type 42 destroyers were formidable ships when they entered service. *Exeter* was commissioned in September 1980 and is seen here outside Stanley Harbour in the Falklands with Mount Kent in the background. Following the lessons of the Falklands War a number of equipment enhancements have been made to this class, although they are not always easily detected as these photographs shows.

Above: *Exeter* has undergone a number of major equipment changes over the years, much of which was done during her 1989 refit. The Type 184 Sonar was replaced by the Type 2050 Sonar, Type 992 Radar was replaced by the Type 996 and a new Sea Dart 909 guidance radar was fitted. The 30mm guns were replaced with Phalanx while the Oerlikons have been replaced with the GAM-BO1. In addition, the combat computer system has been vastly updated.

Right: The first indication that a warship might get of a submarine in the area is the moment when the torpedo impacts. To ensure that this does not happen the ship's sonar operators will be constantly monitoring their equipment, while Sea King crews will also be searching. Although the periscope and sensors of this submarine are easy to detect in a calm sea, this will not be the case when the sea is rough and the submarine is some distance away.

Fortunately for the submarine this was an exercise. The flare dropped by the Sea King was to indicate that it had completed an attack, but how many attacks the SSK had already made was uncertain.

Above: The Sea Dart was designed as a surface-to-air missile, capable of intercepting aircraft or missiles from high altitude to sea skimming; it also has an anti-surface vessel capability. Although it is mounted on a twin-launcher, its rate of fire is rapid due to the automatic reloading system. The Sea Dart System is capable of engaging multiple targets simultaneously.

During the Gulf War a pair of Sea Dart missiles were fired at an Iraqi Silkworm missile by *Gloucester*, successfully destroying it.

Below: *Nottingham* was built by Vosper Thorneycroft and was commissioned in April 1983. She has a complement of 280 who are highly trained in their respective departments of Operations, Supply and Secretariat, Weapons Engineering and Marine Engineering.

Right: Two female guards pictured aboard *Liverpool*. During her last refit *Liverpool*'s accommodation was converted to accept up to 27 Junior and six Senior Rates. The Royal Navy currently has in excess of 700 women at sea serving on surface ships.

On 1 November 1993, the Women's Royal Naval Service (WRNS) was formally integrated into the Royal Navy. With that, the WRNS ceased to exist although ratings will have the suffix 'Wren' after their rank (e.g., CPO Wren Smith)

Type 42 Batch 3 Destroyer

Pennant No.	Ship
D95	*Manchester*
D96	*Gloucester*
D97	*Edinburgh*
D98	*York*
Displacement	4,500 tonnes
Length	139.0m
Beam	15.2m
Speed	29.5kts
Complement	297
Armament	(see Batch 1)
Aircraft	1 x Lynx helicopter

Below: A comparison can be made here between the Batch 1 (*Cardiff*), and Batch 3 (*York*), that has the stretched and revised bow plus a strengthening beam.

Left: During her last refit by Devonport Management Ltd, *Manchester* had over 70 per cent of her sensors and weapon systems removed and replaced by new and improved equipment. At the heart of them all is the Ferranti ADAWS 8 with ADIMP, to be fitted to all the Batch 3 ships. This provides an interface with weapons, sonars, ESM, periscopes, radar and navigation equipment. It processes the large volume of data and presents it in a structured form to enable command to be fully informed. This should enable effective counter-orders to be given and successfully conducted.

Below: The design of the Type 42 Batch 3 destroyer has been stretched to provide better seakeeping qualities, greater speed and improved weapon systems. Completion of the last three ships was delayed to incorporate modifications in the light of experience gained from the Falklands War.

Above: *Edinburgh* passes an Arab dhow in the Gulf during her Armilla Patrol deployment. Note the single Phalanx just aft of the 4.5in gun. This was a temporary installation and unique to this ship; she later reverted to the standard two Phalanx.

Below: The arrival alongside is always an emotional occasion for families and friends after a lengthy deployment, especially when it has included a war zone. For the Captain, this is no time to relax as the ship must be carefully brought alongside. This requires a great deal of delicate co-ordination between himself, the helmsman, the engine room and members of the Royal Maritime Auxiliary Service (RMAS) if damage to the ship is to be avoided.

Frigates

The frigate is the general purpose ship of the fleet, the smallest unit that can be deployed independently on a world-wide basis to carry out a variety of low-level deterrent tasks. Historically, the frigate is smaller than the destroyer but no longer is this the case.

Type 22 Batch 1 Frigate

Pennant No.	Ship
F88	*Broadsword*
F89	*Battleaxe*
F90	*Brilliant*
F91	*Brazen*
Displacement	3,556 tonnes
Length	131.0m
Beam	14.7m
Speed	29kts
Complement	220
Armament	4 x Exocet SSM, 2 x Sea Wolf SAM systems, Mk 44 or Stingray torpedoes, 2 x 30mm BMARC GCM-AO3 and/or 2 x 20 GAM-BO1guns
Aircraft	2 x Lynx helicopters

Above left: A Type 22 frigate is seen here manoeuvring sharply to avoid a simulated air attack by one of the Flight Refuelling Falcons. Simultaneously, she will be trying to ensure that her defensive anti-aircraft weapons will not be placed at any disadvantage.

Broadsword and *Brilliant* were part of the Task Force sent to the South Atlantic to free the Falklands. Their primary role was to provide anti-submarine protection for the Type 42 air defence destroyers. They were fitted with Sea Wolf short-range missiles that proved to be highly successful with their rapid response. On several occasions the first that the crew knew of an inbound air attack was the system warning gong and the launching of the missiles. Such was the success of the ships during the conflict that additional orders were placed above the seven originally planned.

Above right: The GEC-Marconi Shield Tactical Decoy System is fitted to each of the Type 22 Batch 1 and 2 frigates as well as the 'Ton' Class Mine Counter-Measures Vessels (MCMVs) and the 'Castle' Class Off-Shore Patrol Vessels.

Shield is a highly effective, fully automatic decoy system to defend ships from attack by anti-ship missiles. This is achieved by operating in four modes. First of all, the chaff decoys confuse hostile radars by the creation of multiple targets. Secondly, the chaff decoys can be deployed up to 2.5km from the ship, thus causing a distraction for the missile's radar to lock on before the ship is detected. Thirdly, once it is known that the in-coming missile has locked onto the ship, a combined salvo of chaff and IR decoys are launched. This effect is to cause the combined decoy to pass through the field of view and range gate of the missile, and to seduce it away from the ship. The fourth is also used when the missile has locked on and is known as the 'Dump' mode. Here a decoy is positioned outside the missile's range gate and the ship's on-board jammer is used to shift the range gate window onto the decoy.

The Shield system stores a number of successful tactical deployments of the decoys together with their effectiveness. When faced with a threat, the system selects the most appropriate successful deployment pattern from sensor information and automatically launches the decoys in a pattern that will provide the highest probability of success.

Type 22 Batch 2 Frigate

Pennant No.	Ship
F92	*Boxer*
F93	*Beaver*
F94	*Brave*
F95	*London*
F96	*Sheffield*
F98	*Coventry*
Displacement	4,100 tonnes
Length	146.0m
Beam	14.7m
Complement	265–275
Speed	30kts (28kts *Brave*)
Armament	(see Batch 1)
Aircraft	2 x Lynx helicopters

Right: Prior to orders being placed, the design of the last three ships of the original order was modified to increase the length. This was to provide additional space for extra command and control equipment, to increase stability as well as streamlining the bow. The result was that the Batch 2 ships, as they were known, were faster and had a drier foredeck.

Boxer was built by Yarrow (Shipbuilders) Ltd at Glasgow and commissioned into the Royal Navy on 14 January 1984. She was initially used as a trials ship for the new Computer Assisted Command System (CACS1). Power is provided two Rolls-Royce Tyne gas-turbines for economical cruise, while two Rolls-Royce TM3B Olympus gas-turbines provide boost power for high speed acceleration and transit. Combined, the Batch 2 has a maximum speed of 30kts. When running on the TM3Bs only and at 18kts, it has an impressive range of 4,500 miles.

Brave differs from her sister ships in that she is fitted with Rolls-Royce SM1C Spey gas-turbines to replace the TM3B Olympus. Her top speed is 28kts while the rest of the Batch 2s have a maximum speed of 30kts.

Above: The Type 22 frigate can accommodate two Lynx HAS.3, but in peacetime only one is usually deployed. Seen here is a Lynx dropping a Sting Ray torpedo that it would carry for ASW and some ASV tasks.

This autonomous acoustic homing torpedo is fitted with a multi-mode multi-beam sonar and a quiet high-speed propulsion system. A fully programmable on-board digital computer enables it to give a high performance in deep water as well as shallow, where sonar conditions prove difficult.

Left: The Type 22 includes the BMARC 30mm GCM-AO3 in its anti-aircraft weaponry. This twin barrelled weapon system can fire 1,300 rounds/min. It can be used to fire a single round when a warning shot is required for effect during a patrol.

Right: A superb shot of the Type 22 Batch 2 frigate HMS *Boxer*. This photograph shows well the elegant lines of this class of warship.

Above: The final loading of stores aboard *London* while she is alongside at Devonport before she sails on her next deployment.

As the Royal Navy Flagship in the Gulf, *London* handled between 1,200 and 1,400 signals a day. By the end of the war she had dealt with over 45,000 in 40 days and retained 100 per cent availability of all her tactical communications systems.

Below: *London*'s Lynx HAS3 is pictured here on patrol during the Gulf War. Her helicopter flight was largely tasked with her support and that of RFA *Argus*. Due to the wide resources available to the Allied Forces, it was decided that a CONsolidated OPerationS (CONOPS) would be utilised. This required the tasking of a US Navy SH-60 helicopter with the generation of an area surface picture using its excellent radar, processing power and data link. Meanwhile, the Lynx would operate as a probe to identify contacts. If the contact was confirmed as hostile, which would be confirmed using the Forward Looking Infra-red Radar (FLIR) or Electronic Counter-Measures (ECM), the order would be given to engage and the Lynx would attack with its Sea Skua missiles.

Right: The Lynx deployed to the Gulf War had undergone a number of modifications. These included the Whittaker Yellow Veil ECM pod, seen to the right of the fuselage, and the GEC Sandpiper FLIR just inboard. Loral Challenger Infra-Red (IR) jammers were located above the cockpit. This electronics fit gave the Lynx enhanced offensive and defensive capabilities during the conflict.

Opposite page, top: *London* makes a goodwill visit, appropriately, to the City of London with Tower Bridge visible in the background. Displaying some of its weapons is a Lynx HAS.3 with the Sting Ray torpedo and a pair of Depth Charge Mk. 11s.

Left: *Coventry* is pictured alongside at Gibraltar where the Royal Navy and RAF maintain a presence. Once a strategic position for replenishment of warships transiting the Mediterranean, Gibraltar still fulfils a role by monitoring military sea traffic transiting the narrow straits and providing a link in the communications network.

Above: The Plessey STWS 2 torpedo launching system is fitted to *Coventry* and all Type 22 frigates. It is a quick reaction anti-submarine weapon system which presets and launches either Mk 46 or Sting Ray torpedoes. The launcher comprises three tubes and a microprocessor-based processor that takes information from AIO, sonar or manual input. It calculates the target's position and hit probability, then advises the Anti-Submarine Warfare Director (ASWD) who selects the appropriate weapon.

Above: The Type 22 Batch 1 and 2 frigates are now the only Royal Navy warships fitted with the Exocet anti-ship missile. Designed and built by Aerospatiale, the Exocet achieved world-wide infamy in 1982 through the air attacks against HMS *Sheffield* and MV *Atlantic Conveyor* by the Argentinians in the Falklands War. The Royal Navy MM.38 Exocet is from the same family of anti-ship missiles, but is designed to be launched from a ship.

Left: The BAe Sea Wolf is a close area defence anti-missile missile. It is capable of intercepting and destroying high speed missiles under most weather conditions. The launcher-mounted Sea Wolf is fitted to all Type 22 frigates while the Type 23s are equipped with the Vertically Launched Sea Wolf.

Above: Initially, the target is detected and tracked by the ship's surveillance radar and then the Sea Wolf system radar takes over. The missile is powered by a solid booster giving a Mach 2 capability and, once launched, it is guided to the target with in-flight corrections transmitted by a microwave command link. Data is provided by the surveillance/tracking radars or TV system, via the fire control system.

Below: A general view of *Boxer*'s Ops Room showing the banks of consoles that display data from the various sensors, which have been processed through the Ferranti Computer Assisted Command System (CACS). This system reduces the workload by requesting complicated sequences of required information automatically, rather than relying on the memory of the operator. The use of keyboards and light pens have also increased the efficiency and thus command capability, vital keys to surviving in today's increasingly technological arena of naval warfare.

Type 22 Batch 3 Frigate		Armament	8 x Harpoon SSM, 2 x 6 Sea Wolf SAM system, 1 x 4.5in (114mm) gun, 1 x 30mm Goalkeeper CIWS, Mk. 44 or Stingray torpedoes, 2 x DES/Oerlikon 30mm guns
Pennant No.	Ship		
F85	*Cumberland*		
F86	*Campbeltown*		
F87	*Chatham*		
F99	*Cornwall*		
Displacement	4,775 tonnes		
Length	146.0m		
Beam	14.7m		
Speed	30kts	Aircraft	2 x Lynx or 1 x Sea King helicopters
Complement	240		

Below: The four Type 22 Batch 3 frigates are basically similar to the Batch 2 but are powered by the Rolls-Royce Spey SM1A and Tyne RM1C gas-turbines. These engines enable the ship to reach maximum speed in two minutes and stop in just 750m. In addition the armaments have been increased to include a 4.5in gun and Goalkeeper CIWS; four Exocets have been replaced with eight Harpoon anti-ship missiles.

The Batch 3 frigates have a complement of approximately 240, of which 31 are officers. They also have the facility to act as the command ship for an Admiral and his staff for which extra accommodation space is available.

Left: Each of the Batch 3 Type 22s is fitted with a Vickers 4.5in Mk 8 Gun for anti-surface vessel and shore bombardment. Aft is one of two Sea Wolf missile launchers for anti-aircraft and anti-missile defence.

Left: To the left is the Marconi Type 911 Radar for the Sea Wolf while below, at deck level, is a Marconi Sea Gnat system. This is designed to launch projectiles carrying jammers and decoys to distract attacking missiles. To the right is a shrouded Goalkeeper CIWS and in the centre are two sets of quad Harpoon missile launchers.

In addition, being the later builds these ships were able to take advantage of later variants of ESM, ECM, Combat Data and Fire Control Systems.

Left: Seen here fitted on *Cumberland*, the McDonnell Harpoon surface-to-surface missile system has replaced the Exocet missile system fitted to Type 22 Batch 1s and 2s. The quad launchers are fitted to all four of the Type 22 Batch 3s.

The Harpoon missile is programmed with the target information immediately prior to launch. No further guidance is provided by the ship once the missile has been fired. Navigation and altitude are controlled by an on-board computer and final guidance is provided by an active radar homer. Harpoon is powered by a J402 turbojet and has a solid-propellant booster for the launch. It has a range of over 90km. The ship-launched Harpoon entered service with the US Navy in 1977 followed by an air-launched variant a few

Above: *Chatham* was the last of four of the Type 22 Batch 3 frigates built for the Royal Navy. She is similar in size to her previous namesake classified as a World War 1 cruiser, but today's *Chatham* is designated a frigate!

During a spell on Armilla Patrol in the Gulf, *Chatham* was to become the first Royal Navy ship to engage in joint manoeuvres with a Russian warship. The exercise, which was conducted on 21 October 1992, commenced with a cross-decking evolution in which a Kamov Ka-27 'Helix' helicopter landed on *Chatham* and included the transferring of the Task Group Commander from the *Admiral Vinogradov*.

Below: The DES DS30.B gun mounting is equipped with the Oerlikon KCB 30mm cannon, as fitted on the Type 42 Batch 3 destroyers. This gun fires at 650 rounds/min and has a range of some 10km. It replaces the 20mm GAM-BO1 fitted to the Batch 1 and 2 frigates.

Above: Sea Gnat is the result of an international collaborative project to standardise a decoy system that can fire electro-magnetic and infra-red projectiles to distract and confuse attacking missiles. This is a joint US, UK, German, Norwegian and Danish project, designed to be fitted on ships of frigate size and above.

Above right: Part of the function of the Armilla Patrol Task Group is the enforcing of the United Nations Security Council's Resolution 567. This involves the policing of the sanctions on maritime trade with Iraq. In order to fulfil this function effectively, the ship has the UN's authority to check ships that might be sanction breaking. The most effective way for this to

be conducted is to rapid-rope a team of Royal Marines onto the ship to conduct the search.

Rapid-roping is also being used operationally by Royal Navy vessels in the Adriatic for boarding ships. This is in support of the UN where a further embargo exists on the civil-war torn states of the former Yugoslavia.

Below: The hangar is capable of accommodating two Lynx HAS.3s although only one is carried by the Type 22 in peacetime. Alternatively, a Sea King HAS.6 may be carried. Space has been provided on the last four of this batch for the larger EH101 Merlin helicopter when it eventually enters service.

Right: A Sea Skua is prepared for winching onto the Lynx's launcher rail. Up to four Sea Skua anti-ship missiles can be fitted to the Lynx. These have a range of some 15km and enable the helicopter to complete its attack without becoming too vulnerable to counter-attack.

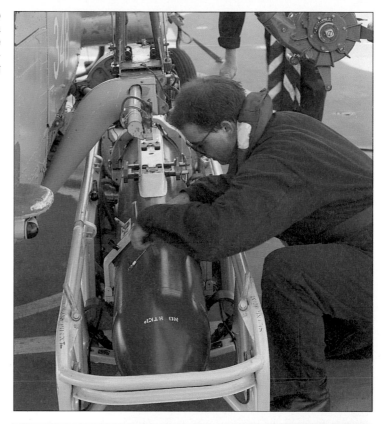

Right: All Royal Navy ships regularly undergo a major refit when they are placed in a dry dock, where much of their equipment is stripped and refurbished or replaced.

Campbeltown clocked up its 500,000th nautical mile while en-route to the South Atlantic in 1992 and can be seen here undergoing a refit at Devonport.

Type 23 Frigate

Pennant No.	Ship
F229	*Lancaster*
F230	*Norfolk*
F231	*Argyll*
F233	*Marlborough*
F234	*Iron Duke*
F235	*Monmouth*
F236	*Montrose*
F237	*Westminster*
F238	*Northumberland*
F239	*Richmond*
F240	*Somerset*
F241	*Grafton*
F242	*Sutherland*

Displacement	4,000 tonnes
Length	133.0m
Beam	16.0m
Speed	28kts
Complement	179
Armament	8 x Harpoon SSM, Vertical Launch Sea Wolf SAM system, 1 x 4.5in (114mm) gun, Stingray torpedoes, 2 x 30mm DES/Oerlikon guns
Aircraft	1 x Lynx helicopter

Below: In the past, a naval frigate was a fast manoeuvrable craft that was required to scout ahead of the main fleet. To keep her weight down she was invariably relatively lightly armed.

The ships of the 'Duke' Class of Type 23 frigates are the latest type of frigate to become operational with the Royal Navy. They are easily capable of this role plus a lot more besides, and by comparison with similarly sized ships of other navies they are heavily armed.

Each ship is manned by up to 17 officers, 57 senior ratings and 111 junior ratings.

Right: Built by Yarrow (Shipbuilders) Ltd of Glasgow, *Norfolk* (F230) was the first of the Type 23s to enter service when she was commissioned on 1 June 1990. Following lessons learned during the Falklands War, these ships have be designed to give a reduced radar signature that can mimic the appearance of a fishing boat on enemy radar screens. The Type 23's construction is zoned so as to reduce vulnerability.

Currently the Type 23 are equipped with the Lynx for ASW, but have been designed to accommodate the Merlin (as shown here) when they become operational.

Right: Thought has been given to reduce the risk to the crew on deck during action: for example, torpedoes can be loaded and launched from below decks. In this photograph, the exit hatches are just visible above the deck-mounted pulley.

Several million pounds' worth of stores and spares are carried on the Type 23. However, periodic resupply in the form of a RAS is required to ensure these frigates are maintained at their peak of readiness.

Below: An aerial view of *Argyll* showing the forward layout of the ship's weapon systems, sensors and radar that utilise the most advanced electronic and computer technology in the Fleet.

Visible halfway up the mast and looking like a ball with three dark areas on it, is Sea Archer. This is a naval gunfire control system that is currently in service on Type 22 Batch 3s as well as the Type 23 frigates. Also known as the GSA8, this automatic tracking technolo-

gy provides the ship with a covert surveillance, automatic search and acquisition plus a tracking and engagement facility against air, surface and shore-based targets.

Below right: Included in the armoury of Type 23 frigates are the 4.5in Gun, 32 Vertical Launch Sea Wolf missiles in silos, and Harpoon anti-ship missiles.

Right: The Ship's Flight Lynx aboard *Argyll* is checked by one of the ground crew prior to another sortie. Following behind are other ships of this Task Group. Once in service the much larger Merlin will provide the airborne ASW and ASV coverage with a much enhanced capability.

Right: The BAe Vertical Launch Sea Wolf is an automatic, fast reaction, high speed, ship-launched anti-aircraft and anti-missile missile. It is currently fitted to all Type 23 frigates for close area defence. This third generation system is developed from the six barrel conventionally launched system.

The Vertical Launch Sea Wolf has been designed to eliminate the problem of blind spots. Fitted with an additional booster, VL Sea Wolf is launched from a vertically mounted silo. Once clear of the ship's superstructure, the missile turns through an arc of some 90 degrees onto the heading of the target. The booster then separates and the missile intercepts the target at a speed approaching Mach 2.

Right: The 4.5in Vickers Mk. 8 Gun was designed by RARDE and is modelled on the Abbot gun used by the British Army. It can fire 25 rounds/min out to a range of 22km.

Left: One of the pair of DES DS30 gun mounts equipped with Oerlikon·KCB 30mm guns fitted to *Argyll*, pictured during a live firing exercise.

Lower left: The Type 23 frigates are powered by the COmbined Diesel eLectric And Gas (CODLAG) to meet the optimum power-to-noise ratio. The cruise power is supplied by four Paxman Valenta diesel generators. Two of these engines are double-mounted and acoustically hooded for silent operation.

The turbine arrangement is provided by two 37,540shp Rolls-Royce Spey gas-turbines with which they are capable of a maximum speed of 28kts. When operating at a more economical speed of 15kts, Type 23s have a range of 7,800 miles.

Bottom left: Down in the Ship Control Centre the Engineering Officer and his team will be monitoring the power requirements against the current availability.

Below: Being unmanned, the 4.5in gun turret is designed for weather protection rather that anything else. As an automatic weapon, its laying speed is determined by the effort required to rotate the mass of the turret. To reduce this mass the turret dome is constructed of glass reinforced plastic.

Above: The CODLAG engine arrangement enables an impressive acceleration as shown here by *Marlborough*. When high speed sprint is required either one or both Rolls-Royce SM1A Spey gas-turbines provide the necessary extra power. However, this increase in speed also results in an increase in the ship's noise signature. The SM1C was fitted in later builds of the class.

Right: The first eight ships of the Type 23s are due to be retro-fitted with the BAe SEMA Surface Ship Command System (SSCS) at their first refit stage. The Operations Room comprises of 5 Divisions – Missile, Sonar, Radar, Electronic Warfare and Communications.

Left: *Montrose* quietly slips into Devonport on delivery from her builders, Yarrow (Shipbuilders) Ltd of Glasgow, to join the 6th Frigate Squadron. To reduce the radar signature of this class the external structures are angled at 7 degrees to reflect the radar waves upwards, thus producing a reduced return.

Below: Type 23 frigates are fitted with a wide range of electronic sensors, radars and communications. The domed structures house the Marconi SCOT satellite communications antenna, while above them are the fire control directors for the Sea Wolf and Harpoon missile systems and the air/surface search radar.

Below: The Type 23 has a single galley providing food to two dining halls and the wardroom. In these days of healthier eating the cook, supervised by a petty officer (catering), will ensure that a varied but well balanced diet is offered to all members of the ship's company.

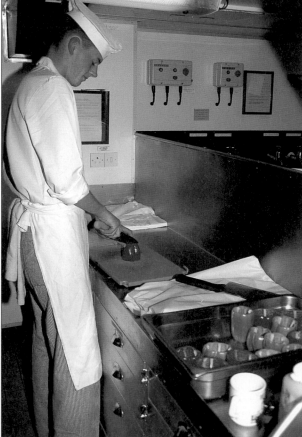

Minehunters and Minesweepers

Underwater mines can easily be laid and are a relatively cheap weapon, rendering passages of water unusable to an enemy. The mines can lay dormant for years until detonated by an unfortunate vessel as it passes nearby. They are also a double-edged weapon in that, once laid to deny access for the enemy, they can also deny access to friendly forces unless a path has been accurately charted.

To counter the threat of mines, specially constructed vessels – often built of wood but nowadays of Glass Reinforced Plastic (GRP) – have been designed to try to deal with this weapon.

Traditionally, once an area is known or thought to have been mined, a minesweeper would be given the task of clearing the mines. The minesweeper would use a towed wire to dislodge the mine and cause it to rise to the surface where it could be destroyed. Alternatively it would use a ship simulator that would trick the magnetic type of mine into detecting a large vessel and exploding harmlessly.

Subsequently, a new breed of Mine Counter-Measures Vessel (MCMV) has emerged, known as the minehunter. This vessel uses a high definition sonar to 'see' the mines and then places explosives on the mine, either by divers or a Remote Controlled Mine Disposal System (RCMDS).

Left: The first of five 'Sandown' Class minehunters was ordered in 1985 and a second batch of six in 1990. However, the latter batch were made available to the Royal Saudi Arabian Navy when the Saudi Goverment decided to place an order. It is anticipated that an invitation to tender for a replacement batch for the Royal Navy will be placed in the near future.

Minehunters – 'Sandown' Class

Pennant No.	Ship
M101	*Sandown*
M102	*Inverness*
M103	*Cromer*
M104	*Walney*
M106	*Bridport*
Displacement	500 tonnes
Length	52.5m
Beam	10.5m
Speed	13kts
Complement	34
Armament	1 x DES/Oerlikon 30mm gun

Left: The 'Sandown' Class are single-role minehunters whose task is to locate and destroy naval mines. Designed and built by Vosper Thorneycroft, the ship has a GRP hull to ensure a low interference with the sophisticated sonar equipment. It will not activate magnetic mines and can resist the shock loads on underwater explosions. The first of the 'Sandown' Class of MCMV was commissioned in 1989 and the last in 1993.

Centre left: Each of the 'Sandown' Class is powered by a pair of six-cylinder Paxman Valenta low-magnetism engines. The sophisticated engine design includes a degaussing system, low-magnetism components and raft-mounted engines with fluid couplings. When combined, they provide a very low magnetic signature.

During minehunting, power is provided by two 100kW electric motors to reduce vibration and noise. Power is transmitted through a pair of Voith-Schneider cycloidal propeller units that can provide thrust in any direction, plus a pair of Shottel bow thrusters which combine to make these ships highly manoeuvrable.

Lower left: The 'Sandown' Class is fitted with the GEC Marconi Type 2093 Sonar. This is the world's first variable-depth sonar which can be operated as a hull-mounted system, or lowered from the ship's centre well. The system will then detect, localise and classify all current and future mine threats.

The towed body, seen here being lowered into the well, has a dual-frequency for both the search and classification capability. This enables it to operate in all sea conditions at a range at least twice that of conventional systems.

Opposite page, top left: All 'Sandown' Class minehunters are fitted with the NAUTIS-M. This is a third-generation Command and Control System. NAUTIS-M interfaces with the ship's navigation, control, sonar and mine-clearance systems to provide a fully integrated MCM system. The NAUTIS-M database is capable of recording 5,000 underwater contacts or features, 100 reference points, 40 tracks, 5 MCM plans and 1 current plan plus 3 hours of sonar swathe or swept path data.

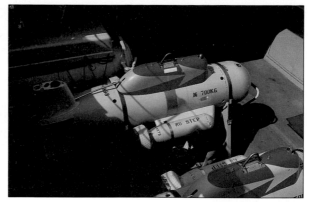

When combined with the unconventional propeller units, NAUTIS-M is capable of automatically following an accurate navigation track, or of keeping an exact station regardless of the wind or tide condition, or of being controlled manually. In addition to being fitted to Royal Navy 'Sandown' MCMVs, NAUTIS-M is fitted to the US Navy's 'Avenger' Class MCMVs.

Above right: The Remote Controlled Mine Disposal System (RCMDS) used by the Royal Navy is the ECA 38 (or PAP 104) mine disposal system which is a French-designed remotely-controlled underwater vehicle. It is used to place a disposal charge close to a mine once it has been located by the minehunting sonar. It can also use its TV cameras to survey the sea bed.

'Hunt' Class

Pennant No.	Ship
M29	*Brecon*
M30	*Ledbury*
M31	*Cattistock*
M32	*Cottesmore*
M33	*Brocklesby*
M34	*Middleton*
M35	*Dulverton*
M36	*Bicester*
M37	*Chiddingfold*
M38	*Atherstone*
M39	*Hurworth*
M40	*Berkeley*
M41	*Quorn*
Displacement	700 tonnes
Length	60.0m
Beam	10.0m
Speed	15kts
Complement	45
Armament	1 x 30mm BMARC gun

Below: The 'Hunt' Class of MCMV are considered to be the largest vessels in the world to be built of GRP. Built by Vosper Thorneycroft (with the exception of *Cottesmore* and *Middleton* which were built by Yarrow), they are also unique in the Royal Navy in that they have a dual role of minesweeping and minehunting, tasks which would previously have required two types of MCMV.

Two Deltic 9-59K diesel engines provide normal power through fixed pitch propellers. A Deltic 9-55 auxiliary provides its power through a special transmission arrangement for the low speed mine warfare operation. Manoeuvring at low speed is achieved by a hydraulic bow thruster.

Left: The stern of *Bicester* is equipped with a wide range of mine warfare equipment. To the left is the float for the Mk. 8 Oropesa. The orange drum to the right is the MS14 magnetic loop, while in the centre is the winch and several cable guides on the extreme stern.

Below: *Berkeley* deploys the Mk. 8 Oropesa with the fluorescent marker visible. She has also prepared her PAP for lowering into the sea once a mine has been located. The PAP is capable of clearing mines down to a depth of 100m. At the stern the MS14 magnetic loop is ready for deployment.

Right: This is the float for the mechanical sweep WS Mk. 8 Oropesa which maintains the correct tension and height for the cable.

Right centre: Divers prepare the PAP for operation. On the front can be seen a light and TV camera, while underneath is the explosive charge. Normally the PAP would be used to lay the explosive but this may also be done by divers. During the Gulf War, eight Royal Navy MCMVs were deployed to the region to handle the threat presented to Allied warships and merchant vessels by Iraqi-laid mines. By the time they returned home over 1,000 Iraqi mines had been dealt with.

Right: Both 'Sandown' and 'Hunt' Class MCMVs are fitted with the 30mm Oerlikon/BMARC DS30B gun which also enables the ship to function as a patrol craft.

Fishery Protection

Protection of the nation's fishing boats has been conducted in one form or another since 1379, when Yarmouth commissioned its own armed fishery protection vessels. Admiral Lord Horatio Nelson was once Captain of the Fishery Protection Squadron.

Today's Fishery Protection fleet is tasked to cover some 200,000 square miles of British fishing limits. In 1991 the Fishery Protection Squadron won the Wilkinson Sword Award for the most valuable contribution to the community.

'Castle' Class

Pennant No.	Ship
P265	*Dumbarton Castle*
P268	*Leeds Castle*
Displacement	1,550 tonnes
Length	81.0m
Beam	11.5m
Speed	20kts
Complement	50 (+ 25 Marine detachment)
Armament	1 x 40mm Bofors gun

Below: 'Castle' Class ships are Off Shore Patrol Vessels with the task of protecting Britain's offshore assets. One of their roles is patrolling the oil and gas fields of the North Sea.

The ship's company normally numbers 50 but this could be increased to accommodate 25 Royal Marines when the ship is being used to counter terrorist threats to oil rigs. In case it is required, a 40mm Bofors gun has been fitted to these ships. Ships of the 'Castle' Class have also undertaken trials for minelaying.

Above: However, most of their tasking is for fishery protection within the UK's 200-mile limit where watch is kept for unlicensed vessels and illegal operation. The 'Castle' Class are equipped with two Avon Sea Rider high-speed craft for transporting the boarding crews. Although they have no onboard hangar, the ships have a large flight deck capable of operating helicopters which can range in size up to, and including, the Sea King.

An inspection party board a trawler to check the catch for size and species of fish, and for illegal mesh sizes of nets on behalf of the Ministry of Agriculture, Fisheries and Food (MAFF). While it is likely that the captain would only report infringements, he is empowered to arrest and escort the trawler's crew and vessel to a harbour in the event of serious transgressions.

The 'Castle' Class of ship has been designed for lengthy patrols and has an endurance of five weeks. With this in mind, the area of operation for these two ships has been extended to include the Falkland Islands. This has been conducted on an alternating basis, with one ship operating around the UK while the other is in the South Atlantic.

'Island' Class

ennant No.	Ship
P277	*Anglesey*
P278	*Alderney*
P297	*Guernsey*
P298	*Shetland*
P299	*Orkney*
P300	*Lindisfarne*
Displacement	998 tonnes
Length	59.5m
Beam	10.97m
Speed	16.5kts
Armament	1 x 30mm DES/Oer-likon gun

Complement	36 (+ Marine detach-ment)

Below: The 'Island' Class of Offshore Patrol Vessels were first commissioned in 1978. With a ship's company of 36, each of these vessels can be seen patrolling the UK's territorial waters on the look-out for illegal fishing. They are also responsible for the protection of the oil and gas installations, for which a party of Royal Marines may be embarked. Ships of this class have large storage facilities sufficient for five weeks at sea. During this time the ship could travel 7,000 miles at 12kts, although they have a maximum speed of 16.5kts.

In time of conflict they would be used to provide defence of the ports and anchorages, and support of MCMVs and coastal convoys for which they are fitted with a 30mm gun. Illustrated is *Shetland*, when fitted with a 40mm Bofors gun.

Patrol and Training Craft

The role of the patrol craft is to maintain the integrity of national waters. Two classes of vessel are utilised to fulfil this task. During peacetime, the role is combined with training.

In home waters around the UK the 'Archer' Class is operated by the University Royal Naval Units (URNU). These have been supplemented by four training craft previously operated by the Royal Naval Auxiliary Service. Two craft are based in Gibraltar where they provide a rescue service in addition to the patrol duties.

Oversea, the 'Peacock' Class of large patrol craft were ordered to replace the withdrawn Ton Class vessels. 75% of the cost was paid by the Hong Kong

'Archer' Class

Pennant No.	Ship
P264	*Archer*
P270	*Biter*
P272	*Smiter*
P273	*Pursuer*
P279	*Blazer*
P280	*Dasher*
P291	*Puncher*
P292	*Charger*
P293	*Ranger*
P294	*Trumpeter*
A153	*Example*
A154	*Explorer*
A163	*Express*
A167	*Exploit*
Displacement	49 tons
Length	20.8m
Beam	5.8m
Speed	20kts
Complement	14

Below: The 'Archer' Class was originally ordered from Watercraft but, when the company went into liquidation, the order was completed by Vospers. The ten vessels of this class entered service between 1985 and 1988 and are used for coastal patrol and training duties by the Royal Naval Reserve (RNR) and RN University units, and are therefore based at various ports throughout the country. They are capable of a range of 550 miles at 15kts.

Two of the 'Archer' Class are based at Gibraltar for Search And Rescue (SAR) duties.

The Gibraltar Squadron
Opposite page, top left: In 1991 the rescue and target-towing launches became too difficult to maintain and support and were replaced by two P2000 'Archer' Class vessels, *Ranger* and *Trumpeter*.

The two RIB inherited from the RAF were replaced by two Halmatic Arctic 22 RIBs, one of which is a unique boat known as Hull No. 32. It possesses a self-righting capability, a specially designed yoke to house quick-release life rafts and SAR equipment, and is powered by twin Mariner 135hp engines. The 'Arctic' fast rescue boat crews also train daily and practice their skills which include survivor recovery and fast pacing drills (rapid transfer of personnel at speed).

Opposite page, top right: All junior ratings of the Gibraltar Squadron take their turn on the Duty Crew for these boats and their initial training is carried out by the Royal Marines. These RIBs are capable of 40kts and can carry 15 people – preferably not simultaneously!

Government to maintain the presence and provide a back up for the Marine Department of the Hong Kong Police in the surrounding territorial waters.

The Gibraltar Squadron

In August 1985 the RAF Marine Craft Unit No. 1102 became the Royal Navy Gibraltar Squadron. Prior to this, the RAF had marine craft units all around the coast of the UK operating air-sea rescue launches with the purpose of recovering ditched air crew.

The UK's commitment to SAR for its air crew also extended to its overseas bases, which it still does today. However, when helicopters replaced the marine craft they did so everywhere except in Gibraltar. This was because surface craft were better suited to the secondary and additional roles that they would be required to perform in the Gibraltar areas. These include target-towing and range safety duties.

Below: As a SAR unit, the Gibraltar Squadron is on permanent reaction alert with one vessel at an hour's notice all the year round. When military fast jet flying is taking place within 25 miles of the Rock, this notice reduces to 15 minutes. The HQ is permanently manned and is linked by flash alarm and hot line to the airport. Out of working hours the duty crew carry bleepers and, although always at an hour's notice, the typical 'silent hours' reaction time is under 20 minutes from scramble to sailing. The Duty Boat has a crew of eight people, which comprises of a commanding officer, coxswain, the engineering officer, four able seamen and one marine engineering mechanic. There are two complete crews and a shore support element of four, making a total Squadron complement of 20 men.

Below right: The Squadron Commander is on patrol aboard the Duty Boat. This puts to sea almost daily to conduct territorial patrols and SAR training. During these excursions sea temperature recordings are taken from various points to assist in the Met forecast at RAF Gibraltar. Radio contact is maintained with the Squadron HQ and Windmill Hill Signal Station, reporting any unusual activities.

In addition to the primary role of SAR, the Squadron performs a variety of other functions. The strategic position of Gibraltar makes it an ideal spot for photographic intelligence gathering of vessels passing through the Straits. NATO and national exercises in the Gibraltar area are supported by the Squadron as are warfare courses, deploying ships and all other Army-related exercises. The Squadron also provides a White Ensign presence to these politically sensitive waters.

Left: With an average 1,000 ships per month passing this way, the Straits of Gibraltar are one of the busiest sea lanes in the world. Here, where the cold Atlantic meets the warm Mediterranean, are complex currents and dangerous conditions with very high winds. The Rock of Gibraltar itself creates unusual and potentially hazardous wind conditions for small boat owners, of which there are many. The increasing migration of illegal immigrants from North Africa to Spain in hopelessly inadequate craft has resulted in an increasing number of calls. The potential for SAR work in this area is therefore immense.

'Peacock' Class

Pennant No.	Ship
P239	*Peacock*
P240	*Plover*
P241	*Starling*
Displacement	712 tonnes
Length	62.0m
Beam	10.0m
Speed	25kts
Complement	31
Armament	76mm OTO Melara Gun

Below: The 'Peacock' Class of large patrol craft were ordered to replace the withdrawn 'Ton' Class vessels. Seventy-five per cent of the cost was paid for by the Hong Kong Government, to maintain the Royal Navy presence and provide a back-up to the Marine Department of the Hong Kong Police in the surrounding territorial waters. They are equipped with Rigid Inflatable Boats (RIBs – fast pursuit craft), a small force of Royal Marines and a 76mm OTO Melara Gun. These vessels are frequently used to combat anti-smuggling operations during which illicit cargoes and illegal immigrants are often caught after a high speed chase.

Survey Vessels

The Royal Navy has a small fleet of survey vessels which are used for hydrographic operations world-wide. In addition to determining water depth and dangers to navigation, these vessels measure tidal streams and the position of all objects of interest to the mariner. They would also determine the nature of the seabed and coastline as well as observing meteorological and marine phenomena.

'Hecla' Class

Pennant No.	Ship
A133	*Hecla*
A138	*Herald*
Displacement	2,510 tonnes
Length	79.2m
Beam	15.0m
Speed	14kts
Complement	115/128

Right: *Hecla* was built by Yarrow at Blythswood and commissioned in June 1965. She was the Royal Navy's first combined hydrographic and oceanographic vessel. Ships of the class has been designed to operate for long periods away from shore support and are fitted with an extensive range of sensors, sounders and other measuring equipment, as well as computerised data logging.

Fitted with a flight deck and hangar, these vessels can operate a Lynx helicopter. They also have a secondary role of MCM support ship. During the Falklands War, *Herald* and *Hecla* became hospital ships along with the *Uganda*.

'Roebuck' Class

Pennant No.	Ship
A130	*Roebuck*
Displacement	1,400 tonnes
Length	64.0m
Beam	13.0m
Speed	15kts
Complement	46

Above: *Roebuck* is a coastal survey vessel designed for undertaking hydrographic surveys to the highest standard on the continental shelf region. She is fitted with the Hyperfix and transponder positioning systems and the Type 2033BB high definition, sector-scanning sonar.

'Bulldog' Class

Pennant No.	Ship
A317	*Bulldog*
A319	*Beagle*
Displacement	1,110 tonnes
Length	57.7m
Beam	11.2m
Speed	15kts
Complement	42

Left: Commissioned in 1968, the 'Bulldog' Class of coastal survey vessel have been extensively refitted since then. Originally designed for overseas tasking in pairs, the ships currently spend most of their time in home waters. They have a range of 4,500 miles at 12kts and a maximum speed of some 15kts.

The bridge is divided into two sections: one side is for the conventional operation of the ship, while the second contains all the equipment required for position fixing, digital echo sounders and sonars, and their automatic recording devices.

Survey Motor Launch

Pennant No.	Ship
A86	*Gleaner*
Displacement	25 tonnes
Length	16m
Beam	4.7m
Speed	18kts
Complement	5

Ice Patrol Ship

Pennant No.	Ship
A171	*Endurance*
Displacement	5,900 tonnes
Length	91.0m
Beam	17.9m
Speed	15kts
Armament	2 x 20mm guns can be fitted
Complement	124
Aircraft	2 x Lynx helicopters

Right: *Endurance* and is tasked with surveying and maintaining a British presence in the Antarctic. Painted a bright red to remain highly visible in all conditions, the previous *Endurance* shot to fame at the beginning of the Falklands War when her Royal Marines and Wasp helicopter attacked the Argentinian Navy and troops on South Georgia during which the Argentinian submarine *Santa Fe* was damaged.

In late 1991 *Endurance* was paid-off and replaced by the chartered *Polar Circle*. With a Pennant No. of A176, *Polar Circle* underwent a number of trials and evaluations and subsequently assumed the name and Pennant No. of her illustrious predecessor.

The new *Endurance* has been built with a strengthened bow to provide her with ice-breaking capabilities. Her A1 Rating certification means that she may cut through 3ft of first year ice continuously at 3kts. For operational reasons she has penetrated 14ft of ice for short periods.

The role of *Endurance* is essentially the same as her predecessor and comprises of Sovereign Presence to support UK policy where other Royal Navy ships cannot go; hydrographic survey operations where a genuine scientific contribution for safe navigation is made and co-ordinated with other nations; and finally, *Endurance* supports the British Antarctic Survey (BAS) team with personnel, logistic transport and helicopter lift for which she is equipped with two Lynx HAS.3 helicopters.

These enhanced capabilities have already had an impact on the BAS team. They have provided support and transport to enable scientists to undertake research in areas which were previously inaccessible due to the harsh environment.

The Royal Yacht

Royal Yacht

Pennant No.	Ship
A00	*Britannia*
Displacement	4,053 tonnes
Length	125.7m
Beam	16.8m
Speed	21kts
Complement	276

Above: HMY *Britannia* is used by Her Majesty The Queen and members of the Royal Family for accommodation when on overseas visits of or appropriate visits within the UK. She also has the facilities to entertain Heads of State as well as providing the administrative and logistical back-up during such visits.

A regular feature of HMY *Britannia's* programme is the holding of business seminars onboard, known as 'Sea Days'. These are aimed at promoting British and Commonwealth trade overseas and enable leading British industrialists and financiers to meet their Commonwealth and foreign opposite numbers onboard in unique surroundings. These Sea Days generate many hundreds of millions of pounds of business. Despite this, *Britannia* is due to be paid off in 1997

Left: Commissioned in 1954, *Britannia* was designed for easy conversion to a 200-bed hospital ship in time of war. Although this was not done for the Falklands or Gulf Wars, she was tasked with evacuation of civilians from Aden when civil war broke out in 1986. *Britannia* co-ordinated the evacuation of 1,379 civilians from 55 nations of which she embarked 1,082.

The Royal Fleet Auxiliary Service

The Royal Fleet Auxiliary Service (RFA) was formed in 1905 and comprises of a civilian-manned fleet owned and operated by the Ministry of Defence (MOD). Its main task is to supply warships of the Royal Navy with fuel, food, stores and ammunition while they are away from base, to enable them to remain operational. The RFA also provides aviation support for the Royal Navy, as well as sea transport and amphibious support for Royal Marine and Army units.

The RFA Service is part of the Royal Navy Supply and Transport Service and is managed from London by the Director of Supplies and Transport (Ships and Fuel). It comprises some 2,600 officers and ratings and as such is one of the largest employers in British shipping. The UK personnel serve under National Maritime Board conditions which have been supplemented by special RFA clauses which take into account their specialised task. This includes replenishment at sea as well as provide that crew staying with the ship should it be directed into a hostile zone. Training for RFA crews follows the traditional Merchant Navy route for basic qualifications, but has a substantial Royal Navy overlay to ensure that they are fully compatible for all operations.

RFA ships are painted in the same grey as Royal Navy ships, but fly the RFA flag which comprises the blue ensign defaced by an upright gold anchor.

Following the reduction of Britain's commitment overseas the number of RFA vessels has also decreased. This has been to such an extent that during the Falklands War there were a number of Ships Taken Up From Trade Service (STUFTS) just to support the RFA operation.

During the Gulf War, 142 merchant ships were chartered to transport 90 per cent of the equipment necessary for the British operation. These ships enabled the equipment to be moved quickly and released the RFA tanker and replenishment ships for the role for which they were designed.

Below: *Northella* is a typical example of a STUFTS. She was originally built as a trawler, but with four other vessels she was taken up in April 1982 to act as an auxiliary minesweeper for the Falklands War. She then returned to her owners but has been chartered once more for coastal escort, including nuclear submarines in the Clyde. She is currently used to provide officers with navigational training at sea.

Fleet Tankers – Large

Pennant No.	Ship
A122	*Olwen*
A123	*Olna*
Displacement	10,890 tons (36,603 tons fully laden)
Length	197.5m
Beam	25.6m
Speed	20kts
Complement	108 RFA + 40 naval air group
Armament	2 x BMARC/Oerlikon 20mm guns

Top right: Ships of the 'Ol' Class of large Fleet Tankers are a major asset to any Naval Task Force. Their primary role is to supply warships with diesel and aviation fuel, lubricating oil and fresh water. The ships of this class have specially strengthened hulls for operations in ice.

These ships are manned by 108 officers and men of the RFA. When required, these tankers can operate two Sea King HAS.6s for the anti-submarine role. For this secondary role an additional 40 Royal Navy officers and men can be accommodated.

Right: The 'Ol' Class carry sufficient quantities of fuel, not only for their own requirements to remain at sea for several months, but also to supply fuel to warships. Well established procedures enable RAS to be safely conducted in all weather conditions.

Below: Replenishment is conducted via seven abeam refuelling rigs enabling a ship to be refuelled on both sides simultaneously. Two further (fuel only) replenishment points are located at the stern, seen here being used by *Newcastle*. This allows up to three ships to be refuelled at any one time.

Right: Civilian crews of the RFAs are required to be able to defend their ship and are seen here undergoing training on the BMARC/Oerlikon 20mm gun against a flare target.

Right: Further anti-aircraft firepower can be supplied by pintle-mounted GPMGs.

Right: VSEL Corvus provides a self-defence system against attacking missiles. The system comprises a launcher, in this case with eight barrels, which fires a rocket to dispense chaff. The rockets, of which one is shown being loaded, would be fired in a pattern and each produces a cloud of metal-coated particles about 1km from the ship. This should be locked onto by the missile during its search phase, causing it to explode harmlessly. Any missile that is not lured will need to be dealt with by gunfire.

'Leaf' Class

Pennant No.	Ship
A81	*Brambleleaf*
A109	*Bayleaf*
A110	*Orangeleaf*
A111	*Oakleaf*
Displacement	37,747 tonnes (*Oak leaf* 49,377 tonnes)
Length	170.7m (*Oakleaf* 173.6m)
Beam	25.9m (*Oakleaf* 32.3m)
Speed	14.5kts
Complement	60 (*Oakleaf* 39)
Armament	2 x BMARC/Oerlikon 20mm guns

Above: The 'Leaf' Class of ships are support tankers which have the dual role of replenishing warships at sea and the bulk movement of fuels between MoD (N) depots. Originally there were five ships in the class which were all designed as commercial tankers. Prior to entering RFA service they underwent a major enhancement of their communications and navigation equipment, and the enlargement of their accommodation. One of the other vital modifications was the addition of the replenishment rigs to enable the transfer of fuel at sea. While the main cargo is engine and aviation fuel, they can also provide some food and stores support.

Apart from *Oakleaf*, all the 'Leaf' Class of ships were ex-merchantmen built by Cammell Laird. They are powered by the Crossley Pielstick 14-cylinder diesel engine which develops 14,000bhp giving a speed of 14.5kts. Each ship has a crew of 60.

Oakleaf differs in that she was built in Sweden and subsequently purchased from her owner in 1985. She has a Burmeister & Wain long stroke engine capable of developing 12,000bhp. *Oakleaf* is fitted with a single controllable pitch propeller, together with bow and stern variable pitch propellers. She is fitted with an automatic power management system which enables the machinery spaces to be unmanned. As a result she only requires a crew of 36.

'Rover' Class

Pennant No.	Ship
A269	*Grey Rover*
A271	*Gold Rover*
A273	*Black Rover*
Displacement	11,669 tonnes
Length	140.6m
Beam	19.2m
Speed	19kts
Complement	47

Opposite page, top: Built between 1969 and 1974 by Swan Hunter, the 'Rover' Class are small fleet tankers, powered by a pair of Paxman Crossley Pielstick diesel engines which produce a combined power of 15,360bhp. This drives a single controllable pitch propeller through a clutch and gearbox to give a speed of 19kts.

Above: The role of the 'Rover' Class tankers is to provide fuel, fresh water plus limited quantities of dry cargo and refrigerated stores. They are fitted with a flight deck and are able to refuel helicopters, although they do not normally carry their own as they do not have a hangar. *Black Rover* is seen here refuelling the fishery protection ship *Guernsey*.

Above right: Ships of the 'Rover' Class are highly capable and can operate worldwide in support of warships, even

HMY *Britannia* on Royal Tours. Each is fitted with a pair of replenishment rigs, with four hoses on each, and thus is able to transfer simultaneously to a ship on either side. If necessary the tankers are able to trail a hose over the stern and provide fuel to a following ship.

Each of the tankers is fitted with a bow thruster unit to assist manoeuvring and all have an additional Paxman diesel engine which is used for auxiliary functions such as cargo pumps and alternators.

Fleet Replenishment Ships

Pennant No.	Ship
A385	*Fort Grange*
A386	*Fort Austin*
Displacement	23,482 tonnes
Length	184.0m
Beam	24.0m
Speed	20kts
Complement	180 (+ 81 RN & RNSTS)
Armament	2 x 1 20mm GAM-BO1
Aircraft	2 x Sea King helicopters (up to 4 can be accommodated)

Above: The 'Fort' Class Fleet Replenishment Ships are designed to be able to replenish warships with naval victualling and armament stores, while underway anywhere in the world. In addition to the transfer of stores to warships abeam, the ships can accommodate Sea King HC4s to provide VERTical REPlenishment (VERTREP) and a flight of two is normally embarked aboard each of these ships.

Both *Fort Grange* and *Fort Austin* were deployed to the South Atlantic and were heavily involved during the Falklands War. *Fort Austin* was the first British ship to sail for the South Atlantic and had embarked the Royal Marines and Wessex helicopters that were later to recapture South Georgia.

Below: It is normal for any Royal Navy Task Force to include at least one RFA in the group. This enables the warships to proceed with their tasking without the need to plan and conduct time-absorbing port visits for fuel and stores. It also means that the fuel and stores are taken from the UK, thus the cash for these items is spent within the UK.

Here *Fort Austin* can be seen positioned abeam of *Invincible* ready for a RAS.

Right: The RAS can take several forms. Depending on the circumstances, the RFA's Sea Kings would transfer stores by VERTREP. In times of conflict this can be used for transferring urgently required stores and provisions when ships are some distance apart, and probably not due for a RAS for another day or two. In peacetime VERTREP is often used during a RAS to provide extra carrying capacity.

In the foreground of this picture the stores can be seen crossing over by jackstay during a conventional RAS, while the 845 Squadron Sea King HC.4 is about to depart during a VERTREP lift.

Right: Each of these ships is capable of carrying large quantities of stores in each of its four holds. Handling is by forklift trucks and pallet transporters, with lifts and cranes providing vertical movement. A 'Clearway' system enables the palleted load to be rapidly moved to all the replenishment points as well as to the flight deck lift.

Below: An additional function of the RFA ships is to provide a refuelling point for helicopter operations. Here, painted in desert camouflage, Sea King HC4s of 846 Squadron land on *Fort Grange* for refuelling during a transit while on operations in the Gulf.

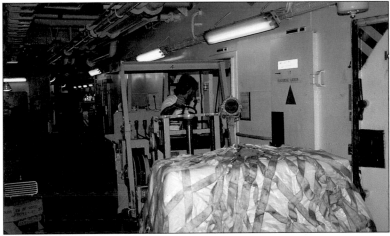

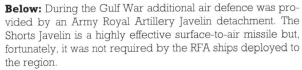

Below: During the Gulf War additional air defence was provided by an Army Royal Artillery Javelin detachment. The Shorts Javelin is a highly effective surface-to-air missile but, fortunately, it was not required by the RFA ships deployed to the region.

Left: With so many nationalities operating warships and aircraft in the confined area of the Gulf, the Sea Kings of RFAs were painted with the Union Jack. This practise has remained and a number of Royal Navy helicopters can be seen with these markings applied.

After the Gulf War, *Fort Grange* was re-deployed to Bangladesh for Operation 'Manna'. A hurricane had devastated the area and large quantities of people and food were moved by the Sea Kings of 846 Squadron and the smaller ship's craft.

Below: A Sea King HAS.6 of 814 Squadron delivers a pallet to *Fort Grange*. The long pole held by one the ground handlers is to grab the lifting strop and to discharge the static electricity built up by the helicopter during flight.

Bottom: *Fort Austin* seen at anchor in the Red Sea with *Newcastle* nearby, returning home after the Orient '92 deployment to the Far East.

Auxiliary Oiler – Replenishment

Pennant No.	Ship
A387	*Fort Victoria*
A388	*Fort George*
Displacement	31,581 tonnes (*Fort Victoria* 33,675 tonnes)
Length	204.0m
Beam	30.4m
Speed	20kts
Complement	102 (+178 RN, FAA and RNSTS)
Armament	1 x 30mm gun.
Aircraft	3 x Sea King helicopters

Right: The latest additions to the RFA Fleet are the Auxiliary Oiler – Replenishment (AOR) ships. Designed as a single-stop replenishment vessel, *Fort George* (illustrated) and *Fort Victoria* represent the latest concept in Royal Navy RAS.

Powered by two Crossley Pielstick PC2 diesel engines capable of developing 23,680bhp, driving a pair of fixed blade propellers through single reduction gearboxes, these ships are capable of 20kts. They are also equipped with six diesel generators producing 1.6MW each. These are located in unmanned machinery spaces, together with cargo and ballast spaces, and are remotely operated and controlled with the aid of computers.

Below: Five RAS stations are available on the AORs. Two dual-purpose to port and a second pair to starboard, plus an astern refuelling reel. Each of the dual purpose stations is fitted with a new high performance rig which is capable of transferring fuel and stores loads of up to two tonnes independently from a single station.

A total cargo capacity of 12,500cu m is available for liquid storage of fuel, lubricating oil and fresh water. In addition, a further 6,200cu m is for solid stores including refrigerated stores and ammunition. The AORs are equipped with a range of handling equipment including fork lift trucks, lifts and cranes to expedite the movement of the stores.

The AORs are operated by an RFA complement of 100 plus two Hong Kong laundrymen. In addition nine officers and 15 industrial personnel from the Supply and Transport provide the stores management and handling. A Royal Navy permanent complement of one officer and 31 ratings operate the military equipment, and a further 29 officers and 93 ratings can be embarked to operate and maintain the flying operations.

The large flight deck and hangar enable the AORs to operate three Sea Kings – and later the replacement Merlin – in the VERTREP role. Facilities and supplies exist for helicopter maintenance.

Fleet Replenishment – 'Regent' Class

Pennant No.	Ship
A480	*Resource*
Displacement	23,256 tonnes
Length	195.1m
Beam	23.5m
Speed	20kts
Complement	134 (+ 48 RNSTS and RN)
Armament	2 x 20mm Oerlikon guns may be fitted

Left: *Resource* is a naval armament stores vessel which also has space for a range of general stores and food, for which some holds are temperature controlled. Commissioned in 1967 she was placed on reserve in 1991. Following the troubles in the former Yugoslavia, *Resource* has been tasked for duties spending much of her time at the Croatian port of Split.

Aviation Training Ship

Pennant No.	Ship
A135	*Argus*
Displacement	28,081 tonnes
Length	175.0m
Beam	30.4m
Speed	18kts
Complement	107 (capable of carrying up to 750 troops)
Armament	4 x 30mm guns can be fitted
Aircraft	6 x Sea King helicopters

Left: *Argus* was built as the ro-ro containership MV *Contender Bezant*. She saw service during the Falklands War in 1982 and was subsequently purchased by the MOD in 1984. Converted in Belfast by Harland and Wolff, she returned to service in 1988 in the role of Aviation Training Ship (ATS).

The purpose of the ATS is to provide a platform at sea for the training of helicopter aircrews, together with onboard handling and maintenance. Without an ATS and with only two carriers operational at any one time (one always being in refit), the amount of carrier time available for operational tasking would be severely cut. This would drastically reduce the capabilities of the carriers to meet their commitments.

Top left: During her conversion, *Argus* was fitted with a dedicated Operations Room which is equipped with monitors for the 994 Air Search Radar and the 1006 Navigational and Helicopter Control Radar. She also has secure communications as well as EW capabilities and a Tactical Data Link. Sea Gnat chaff launchers have been fitted and provision made for the fitting of four 30mm close range defensive weapons.

Top right: During Operation 'Granby', *Argus* was given the new role of Primary Casualty Receiving Ship (PCRS) and to this end a hospital was constructed inside her No 1 hangar in just three weeks at Devonport Dockyard. The facility provided 100 beds of which 10 were for Intensive Care and 14 for High Dependancy patients. The whole unit was sealed to

enable it to function in an NBC environment. The hospital was manned by a team of 23 doctors and dentists, supported by 70 nurses and technicians.

During war conditions a hospital ship remains well out of the immediate combat zone. It is unarmed, painted white with a red cross and protected under the Geneva Convention. However, the PCRS task given to *Argus* was for her to sail with the fleet during any action. For this she was fitted with 30mm and 20mm guns for self-defence and retained her normal Royal Navy grey colour scheme.

This was as a direct result of experience gained during the Falklands War which showed that casualties were less likely to survive unless they were treated quickly. *Argus* therefore remained close to the Task Force, equipped with

four pink-camouflaged Sea King HC.4s from 846 Squadron.

Above left: With her own helicopters, *Argus* would be able to react quickly to any emergency. She could recover the casualties, treat and stabilise them before they were airlifted back to a Field Hospital, and then the onward flight home to the UK.

The stretcher bearers were Royal Marines bandsmen and medics would undertake a preliminary check on the nature of the casualty to expedite their treatment.

Above: Although ostensibly flying ambulances, the Sea Kings of 846 Squadron were armed with GPMGs for self-defence as their role is not covered by the Geneva Convention.

Left: Fortunately *Argus* was not required for any major casualty treatment. However, almost as soon as she had returned home a new role was found for her – that of vehicle and helicopter transport.

Vehicles were stored below deck in the hangars while the flight deck was crammed with Sea Kings still sporting the Allied markings from the Gulf War. Together with Lynx and Gazelles, *Argus* set sail from Portsmouth with a party of Royal Marines to police Northern Iraq and protect the Kurds from attacks by Saddam Hussein's army.

Centre left: On 11 November 1992, four Sea Kings of 845 Squadron took off from their base at RNAS Yeovilton to commence a similar transit. Again, they would be joining *Argus* which would be carrying a number of white vehicles in addition to the helicopters.

This time the role of 845 Squadron is to provide a CASualty EVACuation (CASEVAC) capability for the British troops in Bosnia (UNBRITFOR). Since their arrival much of their work has involved airlifting civilian casualties.

Lower left: The 845 Squadron detachment is based at Divulje Barracks just outside Split in Croatia. It has been the longest serving British unit in the region.

Right: Each of the Sea Kings were painted in the United Nations colours of overall white and, with typical naval humour, were also given a blue berret.

Argus has five helicopter landing spots, each with fuel and secure communications in the form of 'telebrief'. Two 20-tonne aircraft lifts enable Sea Kings, Lynx, and later Merlins, to be accommodated in the four hangars below. She is also capable of operating the Sea Harrier. *Argus* is fitted with a 25-tonne crane which, apart from being useful to assist in recovering any ditched aircraft, can support a replenishment rig to provide fuel to other vessels while underway. She carries 1,100 tonnes of AVCAT and 5,300 tonnes of DIESO of which 3,300 tonnes can be issued through a crane rig while underway if required.

Right: A helicopter can be vulnerable to variety of weapons when flying over potentially hostile territory. The fact that the Sea King is painted white and has the letters 'UN' painted on it would appear to have little effect to the militia gunmen in Bosnia.

To provide some protection against the surface-to-air missile threat, a mixture of Pains Wessex Flare/IR 118 Mk 11 and chaff have been fitted. These have been designed to distract the guidance systems of any missiles that might be fired at them. Here the armourers prepare the flare launchers prior to flying.

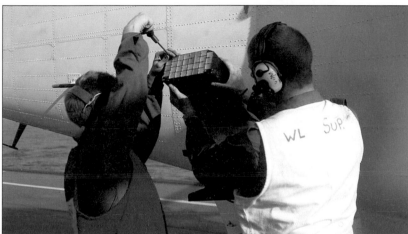

Left: Loaded launchers are mounted towards the rear of the Sea King and the usual configuration is for a pair of flares and chaff on either side.

Below: A Sea King of 845 Squadron fires off its flares in a short sequence. The crew of the helicopter would be keeping a constant lookout at all times when overflying potentially hostile areas.

Left: Once again, the Sea King HC.4s which are providing a flying ambulance service have been equipped with GPMGs for their own self protection.

Left: A view from the cockpit of a Sea King as it approaches *Argus*. She has her accommodation and office space located well forward and the funnel positioned similar to a small island. *Argus* has a large flat deck area and provides a useful platform for the training of helicopter air crew.

Left: As with all Royal Navy ships, the RFA vessels conduct numerous exercises which will prepare the crew for all nature of confrontations. Fire is a real threat aboard any ship, especially when the cargo is fuel. It therefore plays an important feature in most exercises to ensure that it can be dealt with quickly and efficiently. Here, a member of the crew is using the Thermal Imaging Camera (TIC) to look through dense smoke in the search for survivors.

Members of 845 Squadron test-fire their rifles and machine gun aboard *Argus* while en-route to Yugoslavia. Although they were to be conducting UN peacekeeping duties, experience has shown that in order to remain credible they must maintain an effective form of defence.

Forward Repair Ship

Pennant No.	Ship
A132	*Diligence*
Displacement	10,765 tonnes
Length	112.0m
Beam	20.5m
Speed	15.5kts
Armament	4 x 1 20mm GAM-BO1 mountings
Complement	41 (+ 90 RN)

Right: *Diligence* was built originally as the MV *Stena Inspector* and was completed in 1981 as a multi-purpose support ship for the oil rigs in the North Sea. In 1982 she was chartered by the MoD as a fleet repair ship for use in the Falklands War and was purchased from Stena the following year. A number of modifications followed, including the removal of the diving gear and the construction of workshops and additional accommodation. In addition to the repair and maintenance facilities, *Diligence* can provide electrical power, fuel and fresh water.

Following a period in the Gulf, *Diligence* returned to the Falklands where she now provides an invaluable facility for the British warships and RFAs in the South Atlantic, as well as for *Endurance*. A flight deck is fitted which can accept any size of helicopter up to and including the Chinook.

Landing Ship – Logistic (LSL)

Pennant No.	Ship
L3004	*Sir Bedivere*
L3005	*Sir Galahad*
L3027	*Sir Gerraint*
L3036	*Sir Percival*
L3505	*Sir Tristram*
Displacement	5,771 tonnes (*Sir Tristram* 6,455 tonnes, *Sir Galahad* 8,751 tonnes)
Length	125.8m (*Sir Tristram* 135.0m, *Sir Galahad* 140.0m)
Beam	17.7m (*Sir Tristram* 18.2m, *Sir Galahad* 19.5m)
Speed	17/18 kts
Complement	65 (*Sir Tristram* 54, *Sir Galahad* 53 + 340 troops)
Armament	2 x 20mm guns can be fitted

Above: The RFA LSLs provide the Royal Marines and Army with a large capacity vessel for transporting their vehicles and equipment. They have the capability to be beached and are fitted with large bow doors to facilitate the disembarking of the vehicles.

Below: Due to the risk of damage to the hull it is usual for the LSL to have Mexiflotes strapped to one or both sides. This will enable vehicles to be driven out of the tail and onto the Mexiflote for delivery ashore.

Sir Tristram was damaged during the Falklands War but returned to service in late 1985, following extensive repairs and the stretching of her length by 29ft by Tyne Ship Repairers. *Sir Galahad* is a new ship, built by Swan Hunter to replace the original which was sunk in deep water off the Falklands as a war grave. Entering service in 1988 she is larger and much more capable than the others of her class.

Royal Maritime Auxiliary Service

The origins of the Royal Maritime Service (RMAS) date back to the days of Samuel Pepys when a civilian-manned service provided the support functions to the Fleet on its return to harbour. These included the supply of guns, ammunition and stores as well as repairs and shipbuilding.

This tradition is continued today by the RMAS, but its scope has been enlarged with the amalgamation of a number of other functions. These include the Port Auxiliary Service and separate services covering ocean tugs, cable ships, certain trials vessels, and the mooring and salvage service.

Today, the RMAS is responsible for the marine services provided to the Royal Navy at the various naval bases, some shore establishments mainly in UK waters, and at Gibraltar. In addition some RMAS vessels have been deployed as far afield as Icelandic waters and the Falkland Islands.

The RMAS has its own diving section which may work in conjunction with the salvage or mooring departments. They also can be required to carry out ships' husbandry tasks, such as hull cleaning or the occasional freeing of fouled propellers.

RMAS is responsible for the salvage of HM ships and naval auxiliaries as required at any location. It is also responsible for the salvage of any wrecks or

Right: RMAS vessels are immediately identified by their black-painted hulls with buff superstructure. The range of vessels includes the large trials vessels and ocean-going tugs, through to the small 'water tractors', harbour craft and barges. Roles range from transporting personnel around the harbour, to cleaning fuel tanks and bilges, and providing pilots.

'R' Class Tugs

Pennant No.	Ship
A361	*Roysterer*
A366	*Robust*
A502	*Rollicker*
Displacement	1,815 tonnes
Length	54.3m
Beam	6.4m
Speed	15kts
Complement	28

Right: The 'R' Class was based on a commercial ocean-going tug which was re-designed for the dual role incorporating harbour tug. This re-design involved the shortening of the hull by 30ft. *Roysterer* was the first of the class and was commissioned in 1972.

These large tugs are capable of recovering/towing large ships across oceans. They are also used for the cold movement (where the manoeuvre is made without power from the ship under tow) of large ships and RFAs, assisted by tugs. These vessels also undertake a range of general work around the harbour as well as some trials.

casualties of any origin within the limits of Royal Dockyard ports. The recovery of British military aircraft which have crashed around the UK is also conducted by the RMAS for the investigation team, and occasionally they are involved in commercial salvage. The RMAS has a mooring section which is responsible for the laying and maintaining of all MoD moorings, bombing targets and navigation marks.

To assist in the trials and evaluation of new weapons for the Royal Navy, the RMAS operates a small fleet of specialised experimental trials vessels and underwater research vessels which are fitted with sophisticated equipment and laboratories.

'Adept' Class Tugs			
Pennant No.	Ship	A227	*Careful*
		A228	*Faithful*
A221	*Forceful*	A231	*Dexterous*
A222	*Nimble*	Displacement	519 tonnes
A223	*Powerful*	Length	39.0m
A224	*Adept*	Beam	9.4m
A225	*Bustler*	Speed	12.5kts
A226	*Capable*	Complement	10

Above: The Improved 'Girl' Class completed in 1971 is essentially a water tractor primarily used to move barges and for painting catamarans.

Left: The Twin Unit Tractor Tug (TUTT) entered service in 1980 and is the principal harbour tug in current RMAS service. Tugs of this class are designed to work in pairs to move large ships. Here *Adept* is undertaking a 'cold move' of *Invincible*. A similar class of TUTT is located at the stern. TUTTs are also capable of coastal towing and are also used for towing targets.

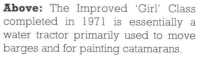

Left: The 'Dog' Class of Medium Berthing Tug first entered service in 1962 and is the RMAS's workhorse. The tugs are used in the moving, berthing or unberthing of medium-sized ships, or for assisting with larger ones.

However, the appearance of this class of tug can vary slightly. In addition two vessels, *Cairn* and *Collie*, have had their towing gear removed and operate out of Kyle of Lochalsh as Range Trials Vessels. *Foxhound* is seen here assisting to cold move *Invincible*.

'Dog' Class Tugs

Pennant No.	Ship
A106	*Alsation*
A126	*Cairn*
A129	*Dalmation*
A155	*Deerhound*
A162	*Elkhound*
A168	*Labrador*
A178	*Husky*
A180	*Mastiff*
A182	*Saluki*
A188	*Pointer*
A189	*Setter*
A197	*Sealyham*
A201	*Spaniel*
A250	*Sheepdog*
A326	*Foxhound*
A327	*Basset*
A328	*Collie*
A330	*Corgi*
Displacement	248 tonnes
Length	28.7m
Beam	7.5m
Speed	12kts
Complement	10

Improved 'Girl' Class Tugs

Pennant No.	Ship
A156	*Daphne*
A177	*Edith*
Displacement	146 tonnes
Length	18.6m
Beam	5m
Speed	10kts
Complement	6

'Triton' Class Tugs

Pennant No.	Ship
A166	*Kathleen*
A170	*Kitty*
A172	*Lesley*
A174	*Lilah*
A175	*Mary*
A181	*Irene*
A183	*Isabel*
A190	*Joan*
A193	*Joyce*
A199	*Myrtle*
A202	*Nancy*
A205	*Norah*
Displacement	107.5 tonnes
Length	17.6m
Beam	5.5m
Speed	7.5kts
Complement	4

Felicity Class Tugs

Pennant No.	Ship
A112	*Felicity*
A150	*Genevieve*
A147	*Frances*
A152	*Georgina*
A148	*Fiona*
A196	*Gwendoline*
A149	*Florence*
A198	*Helen*
Displacement	144 tonnes
Length	21.5m
Beam	6.4m
Speed	10kts
Complement	4

Underwater Research Vessel

Pennant No.	Ship
A367	*Newton*
Displacement	4,652 tonnes
Length	98.6m
Beam	16m
Speed	14kts
Complement	64 (incl 12 scientists)

Left: Powered by a single Voith-Schneider vertical axis propeller, the 'Triton' Class tugs are utilised primarily as water tractors to move the various types of barges.

Lower left: The Felicity Class Single Unit Tractor Tugs (SUTT) were first commissioned in 1973 and are similar in function to the 'Triton' Class. *Frances* is seen here escorting *Trafalgar* out of Devonport.

Below: The Underwater Research Vessel (URV) *Newton* was originally designed for the cable laying role, but is now primarily used as a trials platform, particularly for sonar.

Test & Experimental Sonar Tender

Pennant No.	Ship
A285	*Aricula*
Displacement	1,118 tonnes
Length	52m
Beam	11m
Speed	12kts
Complement	32

Left: *Aricula* is a Test & Experimental Sonar Tender (TEST) which is used in various trials and the evaluation of future sonar equipment.

100ft Fleet Tenders

Pennant No.	Ship
A216	*Bee*
A229	*Cricket*
A230	*Cockchafer*
A239	*Gnat*
A253	*Ladybird*
A263	*Cicala*
A272	*Scarab*
Displacement	417 tonnes
Length	34m
Beam	8m
Speed	11.5kts
Complement	7

Left: The 100ft Fleet Tenders fulfil three roles: *Cricket* and *Scarab* are Mooring Vessels while *Cockchafer* is modified as a Trials Stores Carrier on the BUTEC range, and the other four are used as armament/stores carriers.

Naval Armament Vessels

Pennant No.	Ship
A378	*Kinterbury*
A382	*Arrochar*
Displacement	2,301 tonnes
Length	70.5m
Beam	11.9m
Speed	14.5kts
Complement	24

Left: Naval Armament Vessels (NAV) are fitted with two holds for the transportation of various armaments, such as ammunition and guided missiles, to various locations as required.

75ft Fleet Tender

Type A	Type B	Type C
A83 *Melton*	A207 *Llandovery*	A251 *Lydford*
A84 *Menai*	A208 *Lamlash*	
A87 *Meon*	A353 *Elkstone*	Type X
A91 *Milford*	A355 *Epworth*	A308 *Ilchester*
A211 *Lechlade*	A365 *Fulbeck*	A309 *Instow*
A348 *Felstead*	A490 *Dornoch*	
A381 *Cricklade*	A1768 *Harlech*	
A394 *Fintry*	A1769 *Hambledown*	
A402 *Grasmere*	A1772 *Holmwood*	
A1766 *Headcorn*	A1773 *Horning*	
A1767 *Hever*		

Displacement	150-162 tonnes
Length	24.1m
Beam	6.4m
Speed	10.5kts
Complement	4/6

Right: These are the Fleet Tenders that were commissioned from 1971 to replace wooden motor fishing vessels for use as training tenders, passenger ferries or cargo vessels. They are capable of carrying up to 100 standing passengers or 36 tonnes of freight between ship and shore, as well as ferry services and patrol duties around the dockyard.

The second batch built were the Type B Fleet Tender. These are similar to the Type A with internal variations as were the Type C. The Type X Fleet Tender is similar to the Type A except that they were completed as Diving Tenders. *Messina* is a further variant used by the RNR.

SP Oil Carrier

Pennant No.	Ship
Y21	*Oilpress*
Y22	*Oilstone*
Y23	*Oilwell*
Y25	*Oilbird*
Y26	*Oilman*
Displacement	540 tonnes
Length	42.5m
Beam	9.0m
Speed	9kts
Complement	8

Right: The SP Oil Carriers are employed as harbour and coastal oilers and can deliver 250 tons of fuel to ships that are unable to berth.

SP Water Carrier

Pennant No.	Ship
Y18	*Watershed*
Y19	*Waterspout*
Y30	*Watercourse*
Y31	*Waterfowl*
A146	*Waterman*
Displacement	531 tonnes
Length	40.1m
Beam	7.5m
Speed	11kts
Complement	8

Right: Although they carry a different load, the SP Water Carriers fulfil a similar function to the Oil Carriers with demineralised or fresh water.

Degaussing Craft

Pennant No.	Ship
A114	*Magnet*
A115	*Lodestone*
Displacement	914 tonnes
Length	54.8m
Beam	11.4m
Speed	14kts
Complement	15

Above: The '*Magnet*' Class of Degaussing Vessels is specially equipped to demagnetise submarines to reduce their magnetic signature and thus lower their chances of detection.

Torpedo Recovery Vessels
'Torrid' Class

Pennant No.	Ship
A127	*Torrent*
Displacement	780 tonnes
Length	49.4m
Beam	9.5m
Speed	10kts
Complement	18

Below: To enable it to recover torpedoes that have been fired during trials and exercises, *Torrent* is fitted with a stern ramp. A total of 22 torpedoes can be accommodated in the hold while a further 10 can be stowed on deck.

'Tornado' Class

Pennant No.	Ship
A140	*Tornado*
A141	*Torch*
A142	*Tormentor*
A143	*Toreador*
Displacement	698 tonnes
Length	47.1m
Beam	9.6m
Speed	14kts
Complement	14

Right: The 'Tornado' Class of Torpedo Recovery Vessels (TRV) can operate as exercise minelayers in addition to their primary role.

Mooring and Salvage Vessels – 'Sal' Class

Pennant No.	Ship
A185	*Salmoor*
A186	*Salmaster*
A187	*Salmaid*
Displacement	2,225 tonnes
Length	77.0m
Beam	14.9m
Speed	15kts
Complement	17 (+ 27 spare billets)

Right: The 'Sal' Class of Mooring and Salvage Vessels are capable of lifting 400 tons. If required, a submersible can be carried.

Mooring and Salvage Vessels – 'Wild Duck' Class

Pennant No.	Ship
A164	*Goosander*
A165	*Pochard*
Displacement	1,648 tonnes
Length	60.2m
Beam	12.2m
Speed	10kts
Complement	23

Right: Included in the wide range of tasks capable of the 'Wild Duck' Class of Mooring and Salvage Vessels, are the laying of moorings and harbour defences as well as heavy-lift salvage tasks. A total of 200 tons can be lifted over the bow.

Powered Mooring Lighter 'Moorhen' Class

Pennant No.	Ship
Y32	*Moorhen*
Y33	*Moorfowl*
A72	*Cameron*
Displacement	530 tonnes
Length	32.3m
Beam	11.5m
Speed	8kts
Complement	10

Left: The role of the 'Moorhen' Class of Powered Mooring Lighter (PML) is the maintenance of harbour buoys and markers. They also have facilities to accommodate five divers.

Range Support Vessel 'Warden' Class

Pennant No.	Ship
A368	*Warden*
Displacement	749 tonnes
Length	48.6m
Beam	10.5m
Speed	15kts
Complement	11

Left: *Warden* is the Range Mooring Vessel for DRA Aberporth in South Wales and is based at Pembroke Dock.

Submarine Berthing Tug

A344	*Impulse*
A345	*Impetus*
Displacement	572 tonnes
Length	32.5 metres
Beam	10.4 metres
Speed	12kts
Complement	6

Left: These tugs were ordered in 1992 for submarine berthing tasks at the Clyde Submarine Base and are illustrated assisting in the berthing of one of the Trident submarines - *Victorious.*

Submarine Support Vessel

Pennant No.	Ship
A232	*Adamant*
Displacement	79 tonnes
Length	30.00 metres
Beam	7.80 metres
Speed	23kts
Complement	5 (+ 36 passengers)

Right: *Adamant* is a Submarine Support Vessel (SSV) which is used for the high speed transport of personnel and to handle portable cargo. Designed and built by FBM at Cowes, this vessel is an aluminium catamaran powered by a pair of Cummins KTA 19M2 marine diesel engines which each drive a MJP J650 waterjet.

Capable of speeds up to 23kts, *Adamant* has a passenger cabin with 36 seats and a crew mess room, small engineer's workshop and cargo room. She is also fitted with a specially designed transfer system comprising of a 8.1m long aluminium brow which is supported by a constant tension winch. Together with hydraulically operated fenders, this enables transfers to be easily made in choppy seas without any danger of damage to the submarine.

Towed Array Vessel

TAVR

Displacement	32 tonnes
Length	20.1m
Beam	6.0m
Speed	12.5kts
Complement	8 (RN crew)

Right: A total of three of these vessels are used to transport clip-on towed arrays for submarines. They are based at Portsmouth, Devonport and Faslane.

Catamaran Launch

Displacement	20 tonnes
Length	15.8 m
Beam	5.5 m
Speed	13kts
Complement	2 (+ 30 passengers)

Right: This FBM Catamaran Launch is based at Portsmouth and is used as a ferry to move personnel and/or cargo around the dockyard. It is fitted to accomodate 30 passengers. Constructed of aluminium alloy, it is powered by two Mermaid marine diesel engines.

Aviation Lighter
RNAL50

Left: The aviation lighters were originally used to carry aircraft from carriers or ships to a jetty for unloading. This last remaining avaition lighter is moored in the harbour at Portland and its dummy deck is used to train pilots flying Sea Kings and Lynx.

Admiralty Floating Dock

	Pennant No.	Pennant No.
	AFD26	AFD60
Displacement	38,000 tonnes	
Length	115.8m	150.0m
Beam	92.0m	92.0m

Left: Admiralty Floating Dock 60 (AFD60) was built at Portsmouth specifically for use at Faslane and can provide support for Fleet, Patrol and even the Polaris submarines. The dock is also occasionally used for lifting some surface ships.

The dock contains 36 ballast tanks and by flooding these the submarine or ship can float into the dock. Its first customer was *Otter* in 1967 and by early 1994 a total of 610 dockings had been completed.

AFD60 has a complement of two officers, 18 senior rates and 45 junior rates. Their task is to keep the dock at 48 hour's notice for dockings, except during the Contractor Assisted Maintenance Periods when it is extended to 72 hours.

The role of AFD60 will remain until the Polaris fleet is phased out, but after that plans are still uncertain because the Shiplift will provide this facility for the Trident submarines.

The RMAS operate a number of smaller boats for a variety of tasks mainly around the harbour. These include RIBs for Police patrol, work boats, Pilots launch and passenger transport. Some larger vessels include lighters used to transport fuel, stores, ammunition and sullage.

Left: 15m TSL used as a Pilots Launch.

Above: 15m Range Safety Craft.

Right: The 52.5ft Harbour Launch is used for transport around the harbour and entered service in 1965.

Right: The newer 52.5ft (NZ) Harbour Launch is and which used for transport around the harbour entered service in 1970.

Left: This 14m Harbour Launch is also used for passenger transport.

Left: The 11m Harbour Launch can be used for a variety of uses ranging from diving to transport.

Below: The role of the Tank Cleaning Lighter is to provide the machinery and power to internally clean storage or fuel tanks.

Above: Specialist Oil Pollution Craft are kept in readiness for any potential accidents. This particular vessel sucks up floating oil while larger tugs or tenders might be used to spray detergents.

Right: The 250-ton Sullage and Septic lighters are used to remove waste materials from ships for disposal. Contaminated fuel is recovered for use in low grade burners.

Right: The RMAS operates a large number of stores lighters with which it can transfer water, fuel, stores and ammunition easily from shore to ship, for those unable to come alongside for any reason. These lighters range in size from 100 to 500 tons.

Above: A 15m TSL used for security patrol duties and crewed by MOD police.

Below: One of a number of RIBs – operated by the RMAS for various functions. This particular example is used by the MOD police at the Clyde Submarine Base in the security role. It is illustrated here escorting a visiting US Navy SSN, USS *Alexandria*.

Shore Establishments

ATTURM is the Amphibious Trials and Training Unit of the Royal Marines (ATTURM) at Instow **(right)** conducts trials plus research and development of small craft, amphibious craft, vehicles, plant and equipment critical to the Royal Marines role. Part of the trials carried out by ATTURM is to ensure that vehicles are capable of crossing the gap between the landing craft and the shore during an amphibious landing. Tests are conducted driving vehicles through salt water at depths of up to 1.5 metres.

In addition, ATTURM is involved in the training of drivers, mechanics and landing craft crews.

BRNC origins go back to 1857 when the Admiralty announced a scheme for compulsory training together with an examination before going to sea. This scheme was the result of a proposal by Captain Harris and was conducted aboard his ship, HMS *Illustrious,* at Portsmouth.

By 1859 HMS *Illustrious* was proving

too small and was replaced by HMS *Britannia*. In 1861 she was moved to Portland and a further two years later on to Dartmouth. She was joined by the *Hindostan* in 1864 but such was the success of the college that they were also deemed too small and replaced by the *Prince of Wales* in 1869 having been renamed *Britannia.*

During the 1870s, the Rice Committee recommended the building of a new naval college ashore. Plans eventually proceeded and the foundation stone was laid by Edward VII on 7 March 1902. Britannia Royal Naval College (BRNC) **(below)** was opened on 14 September 1905 and is now the home of virtually all basic officer training.

HMS *Cambridge* is on the site acquired by the Admiralty in 1940 for use as a firing range for the large numbers of men required for the expanded wartime Fleet.

The Gunnery School was named HMS *Cambridge* in 1956 and its current role is to provide live gunnery firing for missile operations courses; maintainer training on firing systems and for students from HMS *Raleigh* who have elected to become Missilemen. The establishment is also the lead school for Internal Security, Small Arms and Boarding Party training.

Clyde Submarine Base originated in the Gareloch in World War 1 and was intensified during World War 2 as an operating base for submarines deployed to the Greenland- Iceland-Faroes 'gaps'. The main locations used at that time were the Holy Loch, Rothesay and Campbeltown. In 1958, the Depot Ship HMS *Maidstone* dropped anchor in Faslane bay, mooring off the foreshore of an area of land already owned by the MoD and previously used by shipbreakers.

Following development, the base was commissioned in 1967 and became home for the Polaris Tenth Submarine Squadron and the Third Submarine

Squadron which had been based with the Depot Ship.

In 1984, the entire Northern Development Area of the Clyde Submarine Base was found to be contaminated with asbestos. The volume was such that it was considered too great for disposal in a licensed off-site tip without great inconvenience to the local communities. As a result three large and very contaminated tips were enclosed in sheet-piled walls and covered in reinforced concrete. An additional 150 tonnes of loose material were converted into an inert glass like substance by vitrification on site. This was the first time that this process had been used on this scale anywhere in the world.

The redevelopment of Faslane, at a cost of £1.7 billion **(below),** has been one of the largest construction projects undertaken in Europe. The major part of these new facilities comprise of the Shiplift, Northern Utilities Building, Strategic Weapons Support Building and the Finger Jetty. In addition to these a new 125 tonne crane, a helipad, General Stores Building, a new Naval Technical Department, residential blocks and modern medical facilities have been constructed.

Dominating the skyline at Faslane is the Shiplift designed to raise all classes of submarine up to and including the Vanguard Class for repairs and routine maintenance. The Northern Utilities Building comprises four machine halls, each containing two 3.1MW diesel alternators and two 2.2MW frequency changers for the on board submarine equipment. It is one of the largest diesel power stations on the British mainland. In addition, it contains facilities for the production of demineralised water plus high and low pressure air and nitrogen.

The Strategic Weapons Support Building (SWSB) **(right)** provides a storage area for the Ballast Cans and other Trident support equipment. This includes the Active Inert Missiles that are used to test the various related launch systems aboard the Trident submarines.

HMS *Cochrane* is located at Rosyth Royal Dockyard. It provides the Fleet Accommodation Centre for the Royal Naval personnel employed in the Rosyth area. In addition it provides the general support facilities including Pay and Records, Stores, Catering and social clubs.

HMS *Cochrane* also houses the Royal Navy's fire fighting and first aid training centres in Scotland as well as running courses in the Supply and Secretarial Schools.

HMS *Collingwood*, near Fareham, is the Weapon Engineering School of the Royal Navy. Approximately 1,000 courses each year are run. These range from one day familiarisation to a 4 1/2 year apprenticeship. There are three schools providing different stages of training for mechanics, artificers and officers.

Some 2,500 people, including 1,400 trainees work on the 200 acre site that contains its own accommodation, shops, bank as well as sports and social facilities.

Training is given to three categories of career and pre-joining trainees. This ranges from basic technical theory, through practical mechanical **(opposite page, bottom left)** and electrical training **(opposite page, top right)**, including classroom work to provide a sound background and expertise to maintain and repair weapon systems **(opposite page, bottom right)**. Further training is given on specific weapons system trainers.

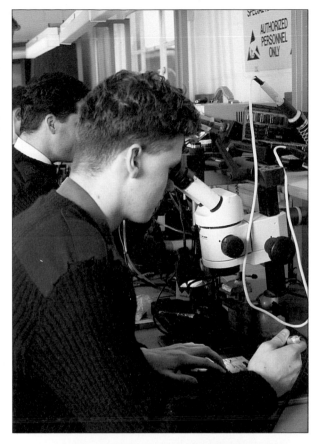

A Type 21 Frigate **(below)** – HMS *Ambuscade* – has been paid off and is seen here in the Frigate Complex when she was being prepared for delivery to the Pakistan Navy as PNS Tariq. The Pakistan Navy have taken delivery of all six Type 21s now that they have been decommissioned.

In 1980 the Submarine Refit Complex was opened by HRH The Prince of Wales which included an additional two dry docks.

In 1987 the management of Devonport Royal Dockyard was privatised to achieve maximum competition and better overall value for money. Devonport Management Limited (DML) has strived to achieve these objectives but one of the results has been a cut in the workforce by some 45%.

In 1993, following competition with Rosyth, the Secretary of State for Defence stated that Devonport had won the contract to refit the new *Vanguard* Class submarines. During the 1980s the quantity of refits to nuclear submarines required the capacity of the two dockyards but this had reduced to the point when only one would be required.

HMS *Defiance* and **HMS *Drake* (right)**. On 17th April 1994 a re-oganisation of the the dockyard organisation structure resulted the Re-dedication of the former HMS *Drake*. The amalgamation of HMS *Defiance*, HMS *Drake* and Devonport Naval Base resulted in HM Naval Base *Drake*.

In addition to the repair work, the move by Flag OfficerSea Training (FOST) together with the Sea Training

RNAD Coulport some ten miles from Faslane is the Royal Naval Armaments Depot **(top)** that currently provides the handling facilities for Royal Navy Polaris missiles and Trident warheads. The Polaris SSBNs have their missiles loaded and unloaded at this facility while the Trident SSBN missiles are loaded and unloaded at Kings Bay, Georgia in the USA. RNAD Coulport is responsible for the attaching and removal of the warheads for the Trident missiles. The Polaris and Trident submarines can each accommodate 16 missiles. However, their loading and unloading is discreetly conducted inside a new enclosed jetty. This enhances the boat's deterrent value as it is now impossible to detect how many missiles are on any of the submarines.

Devonport, the dockyard at the port of Plymouth **(above)**, was originally proposed by Sir Francis Drake. It was eventually chosen as a Government Dock in 1625 but abandoned following objections by local fishermen. Eventually, construction of the Royal Dockyard commenced in 1691 with the building of dry docks, stores and accomodation. In 1824 Plymouth Dock was renamed Devonport.

Various facilities have been added to the Dockyard over the years including the Frigate Complex covering the three dry docks in the Keyham Yard which was opened in 1970. It was designed to give 24 hours a day working conditions and includes workshops, stores and office accommodation for 1,200 industrial and 200 non industrial employees.

ed, the submariner will go to sea as part of the crew under training. After a few months of on hands training and success in an oral board the award of the Submarine Badge makes the effort worthwhile.

A submarine is steered by a planesman of which one is seen here being given instruction in the *Upholder* Class simulator at HMS *Dolphin* **(bottom).** This simulator replicates the steering and hydroplane console and the two axis motion system provide a realistic motion simulation of diving and surfacing.

A submariner surfaces in the Submarine Escape Training Tank **(below)** that is used to train for escapes from depths of 9, 18 and 27 metres. This vital training has to be re-qualified after three and then four and a half years.

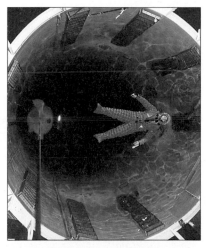

Organisation in 1996 will mean that HM Naval Base Drake will continue to remain busy

HMS *Dolphin* lies on a peninsula that is the western side to the entrance to Portsmouth Harbour. Fort Bockhouse had its origins as a military base in 1431 when Henry VI authorised the building of a tower. However, it was not until 1831 that the Fort was considered complete. The fort has only fired twice in action - the first time in 1642, during the Civil War, when the Parliamentarian Troops captured Southsea Castle. The second time was during WWII when the anti-aircraft guns shot an enemy aircraft down.

The Royal Navy moved into Fort Blockhouse in 1905 to establish a submarine boat station. The name of HMS *Dolphin* was taken from a hulk that was alongside from 1906 until 1923 and used as depot for the submarines.

HMS *Dolphin* is the home of the RN Submarine School. Dominated by the Submarine Escape Training Tank, the school has simulators for the Vanguard and Upholder Class submarines. Once Part 1 and 2 of the course are complet-

Left: HMS _Dolphin._ An instructor lectures students on the Tigerfish Torpedo.....

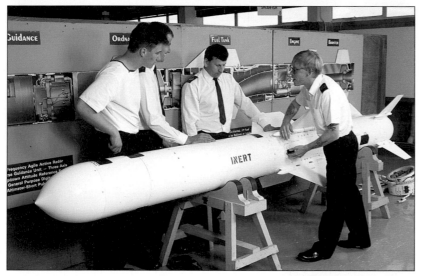

Left:..... and then the Sub-Harpoon.

HMS _Dryad_ (right), located near Fareham in Hampshire, is the home of the School of Maritime OPerationS (SMOPS) which provides training for some 3,200 Officers and 8,300 Ratings each year. Southwick House was originally requisitioned during World War 2 to accommodate the Navigation School when it was moved from Portsmouth. In 1943/4, it was also chosen to house the Operations Centre for the Supreme Allied Commander - General Dwight Eisenhower - as well as the Naval Commander-in-Chief. It was from here that the decision to commence the D-Day Operation was made. Today, Southwick House is now used as he Wardroom and accommodation for Officers and the wall map of the operation remains on display.

The SMOPS courses are conducted with a wide range of sophisticated computer simulators and 'live' training including that for Officer Of the Watch (OOW), Principal Weapons Officer (PWO) and Senior Officers who have been selected to Command a ship on the Officer side. Meanwhile, the Ratings simulators are used to provide realistic training on the various systems of the warships. This includes Above and Below water warfare plus Operations. The Training Support as well as Foreign Training are also conducted at HMS *Dryad* while the communications and navigation elements are held at HMS *Mercury*. In addition, the Maritime Trade, Mine Warfare and Diving training takes place at HMS *Nelson*.

HMS *Excellent* (top) became a Naval Gunnery School in 1830 when a wooden-walled hulk of that name together with HMS *Calcutta* were first moored in Portsmouth harbour. From these they fired their muzzle-loaded cannon across the mud flats in the direction of Porchester.

When the major extensions commenced in the Portsmouth Dockyard in 1867, the spoil was dumped between the mud flats known as Whale Island and Little Whale Island. Over the following 28 years the build up of this excavated earth resulted in Whale Island as is known today.

At that, time gunnery techniques were developing rapidly as did the number of persons requiring training. The hulks soon became unsuitable and

the Gunnery School moved onto the Island.

Whale Island was commissioned as HMS *Excellent* and used as a firing range. Building construction commenced in 1884 and many of these still stand. HMS *Excellent* was de-commissioned in 1985 with much of the training having been transferred to HMS Dryad in 1974.

HMS *Excellent* was re-commissioned in 1994 as the Royal Navy's latest purpose-built modern naval general training establishment. Everyone who joins the Royal Navy will, at some stage in his or her career, pass through HMS *Excellent*.

Amongst the units now located are the RN School of Leadership and Management, the Pheonix NBCD School, RN Regulating School, the RN Military Training School and the HQ of the Portsmouth Command Field Gun. In addition there are a number of lodger units including the harbour training ship HMS *Bristol*, RN Drug and Alcohol Education Unit, RNR Solent Training Centre and the recently completed new Royal Marines HQ.

RNAY Fleetlands near Gosport provides a major servicing, repair and modification facility for the helicopters of all three services. One of its current tasks is the modifying of Army Lynx AH.1 to AH.7 and immmminently the upgrading the Royal Navy Lynx from HAS.3 to HAS.8.

An indication of the capability and standard of work carried out at RNAY Fleetlands was the repairs carried out to an RAF Sea King. In 1989 this helicopter had been taking part in a training exercise when it crashed on a hillside and rolled down the hill **(left)**. Fortunately all the crew escaped with only minor injuries but the Sea King thought to be a write off.

After the crash investigation, the damaged Sea King was delivered to RNAY Fleetlands in a number of pieces where work commenced to remove the crushed nose and cockpit and rebuild the structure. In just over two years work was completed and the Sea King was handed back to the RAF. The cost of rebuilding the Sea King was approximately two thirds of the cost of a new helicopter and saved the taxpayer several million pounds.

RNC Greenwich has been located at Greenwich since 1873 following its move from Portsmouth. However, coins found on the site suggest that it may have been occupied by the Romans between 30BC and AD430.

The site came to prominence following the death of King Henry V in 1422. At that time his brother, acting, as Regent, built an imposing riverside house on the site. Later, King Henry VIII established naval dockyards at nearby Deptford and Woolwich and Greenwich became the scene for the launch and return of many voyages of exploration during the subsequent reign of Elizabeth I.

When William and Mary jointly succeeded to the throne in 1688, they preferred to live at Hampton Court. Mary pressed for the King's House to be completed as a hospital. When the Queen died, William commissioned Sir Christopher Wren to plan the design in her honour **(below)**. The whole project took half a century to complete and the result was a fine hospital and refuge provided for disabled or veteran seamen. In 1869 the hospital closed following the transfer of welfare of the seamen to other means.

In 1873 the Royal Navy College transferred from Portsmouth. The current college comprises several Colleges and Departments which provide training for members of all three services as well some civilians.

The Royal Naval Staff College provides a variety of courses. The Initial Staff Course (ISC) is for junior officers who will be taking up staff appointments while the Staff Course is for lieutenant commander and junior commanders about to take up positions at Ministry of Defence or in command of ships. A Special Duties Officers' Greenwich Course (SDOGC) is provided for ratings on promotion to officer rank.

The Joint Service Defence College (JSDC) was established in 1947 to nourish and disseminate a mutual understanding on inter-service comradeship-in-arms. Without this it would be difficult to provide a successful military force.

The Department of Historical and International Affairs (DHIA) provides lecturing and tutorial support for the above two colleges. In addition to this the DHIA are frequently required to lecture at other Service establishments and colleges.

The Department of Nuclear Science and Technology (DNST) was established in 1958 to provide education and training for officers appointed to nuclear powered submarines. It also for officers and civilians who will be working in support of the Naval nuclear propulsion programme.

HMS Gannet is located at Prestwick Airport and is the home for 819 Squadron equipped with the Sea King HAS.6. In addition to housing the squadron, HMS *Gannet* provides help and assistance to units that frequently exercise off the Scottish coast.

RNH Haslar was originally opened in 1753. It was the first of three established by courtesy of an Order in Council by George II in 1744. The others being at Chatham and Plymouth. It was originally to be built to house 1,500 patients at a cost of £38,000 however, when completed it actually cost £100,000 and was occupied by 2,000 patients. Today, its charter is to run 305 beds but manpower shortages have reduced it to 200. Although all funding comes from Ministry of Defence 80% of its patients are from the local community. In practice, RNH Haslar acts as a District General hospital for Gosport. Its Accident and Emergency Department treats over 20,000 patients.

RNH Haslar acts as a training base for the RN Medical Service (RNMS) and the Queen Alesandra's Royal Naval Nursing Service (QARNNS). One of its primary roles is the preparing of personnel for a wartime role as a Medical Auxiliary (MA) who are the backbone of the RNMS. The MA is unique to the Royal Navy, they are fully trained paramedics who are able to work single handed in any situation.

HMS Heron atRNAS Yeovilton **(top right)** was commissioned on 18 June 1940 as a base for naval fighter aircraft. This remains true for the airfield with 800, 801 and 899 Squadrons that currently operate the British Aerospace Sea Harrier FRS.1/FA.2 based here. It has diversified from its fighter role because 707, 845 and 846 Squadrons are also based here with the Westland Sea King HC.4. The Royal Marines are

also present in the form of 3 Commando Brigade Air Squadron that is equipped with Lynx and Gazelle helicopters. The Fleet Requirements and Aircraft Direction Unit (FRADU) are lodgers on the airfield. Its Hunter GA.11 and T.8 plus Hawk T.1s - are operated and flown by Flight Refuelling Aviation to provide a range of target duties for ships crews.

HMS *Heron* is the flagship of the Flag Officer Naval Aviation and as such the HQ Flight, Heron Flight, is equipped with a pair of Jetstream T.3 and a Gazelle HT.2 for communications. Heron is also home to the Fairey Swordfish and Firefly of the Historic Flight.

To enable these squadrons and flights to function they are supported by an Air Department that provides various services necessary to provide a safe environment for flying. In addition the Air Engineering Department provides the maintenance support to keep the aircraft in an airworthy condition. This includes the stripping down and overhauling engines as well as airframes and avionics.

RNAS Yeovilton is also the home of the Fleet Air Arm Museum that contains some 50 aircraft, charting the evolution of the FAA up to the present day. Major exhibition displays portray events during World War 2 and the Falklands War as well as the Flight deck of an aircraft carrier.

RM Lympstone (left) Here potential Royal Marine recruits will commence a 30 week course. This will enable the Royal Marines and recruits to find out if they have the required drive and abilities to complete the course.

The course is extremely physical with much emphasis on stamina building and teamwork. However, class room work is vital if the recruit is to understand the weapons and techniques that he will be using once he has earned his green beret.

HMS Nelson provides support to officers and ratings serving at Portsmouth and their families. This includes, accommodation, food, stores, clothing, pay, medical and dental plus pastoral support.

HMS Neptune is located within the Clyde Submarine Base at Faslane. As with HMS *Nelson,* HMS *Neptune* provides the necessary support for the 3,600 officers and men serving on the Base as well as wide range of recreational facilites.

HMS Ospreys origins began at Portland with the Royal Navy back on 23 July 1849 when Prince Albert, the Consort to Queen Victoria, laid the foundation stone to the great breakwater. Since then many facilities have been based on the Isle of Portland of which training has nearly always been a feature. Seaplanes were based at Portland dockyard in 1917. However, it was not until 24th April 1959 the helicopter station was opened as an integral part of HMS *Osprey* and thus, RNAS Portland was established **(below)**.

Today, RNAS Portland is responsible for the training and operational deployment of the Westland Lynx together with its associated aircrew and maintainers. To meet this role two Lynx squadrons are based at RNAS Portland - 702 NAS for training and 815 NAS for operational purposes plus a simulator. In the harbour a converted aircraft lighter is moored and marked to provide training for Flight Deck Officers (FDO) and other personnel who will work on destroyer, frigate or RFA flight decks.

In addition, RNAS Portland provides a Search And Rescue (SAR) capability for the South Coast. This is provided by 772 NAS with the Sea King HC.4. An Air Engineering Department is also based at RNAS Portland to provide Air Engineering support, manpower control, training and quality control to the squadrons and the disembarked flights. It has a complement of approximately 280 officer and men.

RM Poole (below right) is located on the Dorset coast. It is where trainee Royal Marines Marines undergo their amphibious warfare training. Here they are taught about landing and raiding craft, undertake day and night exercises, learn how to paddle quietly, disembark in silence, carry out the mission and make a quick getaway.

Portsmouth has been at the forefront of maritime technology for many centuries. Being a natural harbour, it is not known precisely when its maritime history actually commenced. It is known however, that as far back as 1194 King Richard ordered a dock to be built. Also, in 1212 King John gave an order to build fortifications to protect the docks at Portsmouth. It is also known that King Henry VII ordered the construction of the first dry dock in 1495.

While it is considered that ships were already being built prior to the dry dock, it is known that nearly 300 vessels have been built since. These have included the Mary Rose that sank in 1545 after nearly 36 years of Royal Navy service and her remains are currently preserved at Portsmouth. Also Portsmouth had become a victualling site for the ships as well as stores for all the requirements of ship builders and refitting as well as munitions.

By 1850, Portsmouth was the largest industrial complex in the world during a period when there was an almost continuous period of naval warfare. The invention of steam power and the Industrial Revolution was heavily felt at Portsmouth with steam driven pumps for the dry docks and later to power the saw mills. The worlds first complete steam powered factory was built here utilising blockmaking machinery invented by Marc Brunel. Before Brunel's intervention, the blocks needed to rig the ships of the time were being made by 100 blockmakers but, once his new machinery was operating, 130,000 blocks per year were being built by just 10 unskilled men.

At the turn of the 20th Century Portsmouth was building larger and more powerful iron-hulled steamships. The revolutionary HMS *Dreadnought* was built here in just a year and a day. During World War 1 some 1,200 vessels were refitted including 40 battleships, 25 cruisers and 400 destroyers. During World War 2 the workforce peaked at 25,000 and 2,548 vessels had been repaired or refitted.

Despite the conflicts since World WarI 2 the defence cuts have seen a gradual shrinking of the Navy Dockyard at Portsmouth. HMS *Andromeda*, a Leander Class Frigate, was the last ship to be built at Portsmouth and was completed in 1968. The Falklands War in 1982 saw many dockyard workers who had just been presented with their redundancy notices work day and night to modify, load and prepare the ships of the Task Force. This included fitting merchant ships with flight decks and guns, and loading the ships with tons of fuel, stores and ammunition. Just prior to this the Government had imposed a series of defence cuts and the Falklands War only provided a stay of execution.

Today the capabilities of the dockyard at Portsmouth is much smaller and leaner following the ending of the Cold War **(right)**. Once a Royal Dockyard, Portsmouth has been re-named The Naval Base Fleet Maintenance and Repair Organisation. The modern ships of the Royal Navy no longer require the volume of maintenance to keep them operational; following the defence cuts of the past there are less of them anyway, although the cuts have also resulted in a higher proportion of their time alongside. Portsmouth remains the administrative home of the Royal Navy and maintains its traditions and many historic buildings. Admiral Lord Nelson's flagship, HMS *Victory* **(lower right)**, remains the flagship of the Commander-in-Chief Naval Home Command.

HMS *Raleigh* is the initial New Entry training establishment for all men and women joining the Royal Navy and Queen Alexandra Royal Naval Nursing Service. An initial seven week course provides a basic foundation from naval domestic details through to traditions. It also includes physical fitness and fire fighting.

The Royal Naval Supply School, School of Seamanship and the Plymouth Command School are all located at HMS *Raleigh*. These provide fire fighting and damage control, NBC defence, shooting and first aid facilities for ships

and establishments. Extensive training is also provided for cadets of the SCC and CCF.

HMS *Raleigh* has a ship's company of approximately 1,000 of which 25% are civilians. Some 1,500 trainees are on courses at any one time with new entries of 100-140 ratings joining each week, 43 weeks of the year. These are split into Command Schools and Squadrons with further splits into Divisions and finally into four classes of 30 trainees each. Each class is then tailored to the different level of academic instruction to meet the training task.

Rosyth was selected in 1903 for the site of a dockyard. 1,200 acres of land were purchased together with 48 acres of foreshore. This site comprised of an area of mud and water together with Rosyth Castle.

The dockyard was designed to have a large deep water basin which

would be available to all sizes of ships at all states of the tide. Outside this basin was to be a tidal basin for submarines and other small craft. Numerous buildings were required including power and pumping stations, workshops and stores. Reclamation of the 350 acres of the site was completed in 1916. During this period some 10 million cubic metres of spoil was removed.

The original plan for a single graving dock was expanded to three and the the last was in construction when World War 1 broke out. To ensure that there were the minimum of delays the Navy supplied some 2,000 ships crew to assist in the completion and the first ship to enter No 1 Dock was HMS *Zealandia* in March 1916.During the period March 1916 until November 1918, a total of 78 capital ships (battleships and battle cruisers), 82 light cruisers and 37 small craft were docked and fitted out at Rosyth.

In 1925 the Dockyard was placed on a care and maintenance basis and part of the base was leased to a ship break-

ers. This resulted in a number of the German High Seas Fleet, which was scuttled at Scapa Flow in 1919, being broken up at Rosyth.

Following the Munich crisis the Dockyard came back into full operational use in 1939. Fortunately t ie dockyard did not sustain a concentrated attack during World War 2 and was able to work on over 3,000 vessels during the war.

Since the war the Dockyard has seen a steady development with the refitting of submarines (including the nuclear polaris and hunter killers and conventional), frigates, destroyers, MCMVs and various support vessels. In 1980 a Ship Lift and Small Ships Refitting Complex was commissioned.

1986 saw the passing of the Dockyard Services Act and Rosyth Royal Dockyard along with that at Devonport saw the introduction of commercial management. Babcock Thorn Limited were selected as the term Contractor for Rosyth and took over the Dockyard

(which remains Government owned) in April 1987.

Following the extensive defence cuts in recent years the number of refits have dramatically fallen to the extent that there was insufficient work for two nuclear dockyards. A competition resulted in all the nuclear submarine work being transferred to Devonport. However, the Government gave a commitment to Rosyth that it would be allocated a substantial programme of surface ship refits over a 12 year period including 18 refits of major ships and 49 others **(above)**.

HMS *Sea Hawk* is located on the Lizard peninsula near Helston in Cornwall, RNAS Culdrose was commissioned in 1947 and is the largest shore establishment of the Royal Navy and the largest military helicopter base in Europe. Its roles are to train aircrew and other aviation specialists, to provide round the clock SAR for the South West Region and to parent the front line AEW and ASW Sea Kings. Altogether there are approximately 3,200 people based at Culdrose, including about 500 civilians together with some 100 aircraft.

Culdrose provides a home for 705 Squadron who provide basic flying training for all the Royal Navy helicopter pilots. Also present are 706 Squadron equipped with the Sea King in the training role and 771 Squadron similarly equipped to provide the SAR. 750 Squadron is equipped with the fixed-wing Jetstream used for the training of navigators.

Culdrose also acts as the parent station for the operational AEW and ASW Sea King Squadrons. The Sea King AEW.2 is operated by 849 Squadron with an aircraft flight embarked aboard each of the three carriers when at sea. The current ASW variant of the Sea King is the HAS.6 and is operated by 814 and 820 Squadrons which would be embarked aboard the aircraft carriers. When not at sea the helicopters from each of the flights or squadrons return home to Culdrose.

Because so many Sea King Squadrons are based at RNAS Culdrose, it is affectionately known as the home of the Sea King. The high volume of flying movements required to fulfil its tasks can match Heathrow movement numbers at times. This has resulted in RNAS Culdrose utilising a satellite airfield at Predannack. When the Merlin is delivered, it will be first operated from RNAS Culdrose.

HMS *Sultan* (right), at Gosport, provides the training for engineer officers, skilled technicians and semi-skilled mechanics to man, operate and maintain the complicated high-powered machinery in today's modern warships.

Courses can be for promotion or aimed at bringing the delegates up to date with new machines and engineering practices, some of which is through the use of simulators. These are varied but include nuclear propulsion courses as well as diesel, gas turbines, refrigeration and air conditioning plant. Others concentrate on specialist skills such as GRP hull repairs. In the ship husbandry school, officers and ratings are taught the latest techniques for cleaning, preserving and painting ships hulls.

Artificers are skilled technicians who have either entered as apprentices or have been selected from the mechanics' stream. Apprentices join after basic training and commence a course that will last 3 years and 4 months.

HMS *Temeraire*, at Portsmouth, houses the Royal Navy School of Physical Training, Directorate of Naval Physical Training and Sport as well as the Fleet Recreation Centre.

Here, all Naval Physical Instructors are trained on a 24-week course. During the two courses per year with an average of 16 delegates per course, all aspects of fitness, sport, adventure training and administration are covered.

HMS *Warrior* has its site at Northwood which was acqired by the RAF in 1937 to house the HQ of Coastal Command. The first underground accomodation was constructed by the Royal Enginers in 1941 and in 1958 work commenced to expand it by a further two floors. This was sponsored and paid for by NATO to accomodate the Allied Commander-in-Chief Eastern Atlantic. This was followed by yet further expansion of in 1977 and 'The Hole' was opened by Prince Charles in 1985.

HMS *Warrior* was established to look after the administrative needs of the naval personnel on the staff of the Commander-in-Chief Home Fleet. Today its role has been expanded to include the whole of the Northwood Headquarters which includes HQ of Commander-in-Chief Fleet, Flag Officer Submarines and the RAF Air Officer Commanding No 18 Group. In addition, the multi-national Headquarters at Northwood houses various NATO senior officers and their staffs. These include the Allied Commander-in-Chief Channel (CINCHAN), Commander Allied Maritime Air Force, Channel (COMMAIRCHAN), Commander-in-Chief Eastern Atlantic Area (CICEASTLANT), Commander Submarines Eastern Atlantic Area (COMSUBEASTLANT) Commander Maritime Air Eastern Atlantic Area (COMMAIREASTLANT). A strong RNR presence in the form of HMS Northwood is also located on the site.

Royal Marines

The Admiral's Regiment was raised in 1664 to fight the Dutch at sea and their gallantry laid the foundations for the Royal Marines of today. The idea of a Commando force was conceived by Winston Churchill during World War 2 to conduct amphibious raids. Although they were considered ideal, the Royal Marines (RM) were already committed and the first Commandos to be trained were volunteers from the Army. Training commenced in June 1940 and RM 'A' Commando became the first operational unit when it formed at Deal in February 1942. At the end of the war the Commandos were reorganised, 3 Commando Brigade (3 Cdo Bde) remained and was absorbed into the Royal Marines in 1946.

Under the new organisation, 3 Commando Brigade consisted of 1 and 5 Army Commando plus 42 and 44 RM Commando. The following year the Army Commandos were disbanded and 44 Commando was reformed as 40 Commando.

Since that time 3 Cdo Bde has been involved in security operations in Hong Kong, Suez, Palestine, Korea, Aden and Cyprus, plus the anti-terrorist operations in the Far East. The Royal Marines have also been involved in many humanitarian roles. It was in 1967, while in Borneo, that 40 Commando was awarded the very first Wilkinson Sword of Peace for outstanding efforts in fostering good relations. Other occasions have included the relief of hostages in Brunei in 1962, quelling a rebellion by tribesmen in the New Hebrides in 1980. Recently, they have been instrumental in securing an area in Northern Iraq for the Kurdish refugees during Operation 'Safe Haven'.

3 Cdo Bde commenced Arctic warfare training in 1970 and has been committed to NATO's Northern Flank covering Norway and Denmark since 1974. Each of the Commandos have been deployed to Northern Ireland on many occasions. Here again 40 Commando received the Wilkinson Sword of Peace.

On 2 April 1982 the Royal Marines from Naval Party 8901, whose task was to defend the seat of government on the Falkland Islands, came under attack from an invading Argentinian force. NP 8901 had only been relieved by one officer and 43 men just 24 hours before. As a result, 25 of the old party were still on the island plus 12 sailors from HMS *Endurance*. A fierce battle followed but in the face of overwhelming odds from some 2,800 men ashore plus another 2,000 on ships, the Governor negotiated a surrender to avoid civilian casualties. By 9 April, 40 and 42 Commando were embarked in the hastily modified SS *Canberra*. They were despatched as part of the Task Force sent to regain

Left: Royal Marines make a characteristic entry with Rigid Raider and RIBs...

Right: ... but Royal Marines are equally capable of being dropped from a Hercules.

the Falklands. One Company of 42 Commando was flown to Ascension Island to assist in the recapture of South Georgia.

Today, with its HQ on Whale Island, Portsmouth, the Royal Marines Command (RMC) currently accounts for some 12 per cent of Royal Navy manpower. With nearly 5,000 men, 3 Cdo Bde is the operational formation and comprises of 40, 42 and 45 Commando of which each, with 690 men, is the equivalent of an Army battalion. Each Commando (Cdo) is made up of three rifle Companies (Coy), each having 3 Troops (Tp) split into three sections armed with SA80 rifles and Milan anti-tank missiles. They also have an HQ and a support company, the latter of which has a mortar troop, anti-tank troop with Milan and GPMG, a recce troop and an assault engineer troop. Integral within 3 Cdo Bde are components of the Royal Netherlands Marine Corps and, when combined, they form the UK/NL Amphibious Force.

In airborne support of the Commandos are 845 and 846 Squadrons with the Sea King HC.4, assisted by the Commando Helicopter Operational Support Cell (CHOSC). In addition, the Royal Marines have 3 Cdo Bde Air Squadron equipped with the Lynx AH.7 and Gazelle AH.1. While at ground level there is 29 Cdo Regt, RA with the 105mm Light Gun and an Air-Defence Battery with Rapier missiles. A Cdo Logistics Regiment provides the essential stores, ammunition, food and fuel, as well as being able to operate a major medical facility. There is also 59 Independent Cdo Sqn RE, 539 Assault Sqn, the Special Boat Sqn (SBS), Brigade Patrol Group, Brigade HQ and Signals Sqn, plus a Royal Marines Reserve Coy.

Support for amphibious operations is provided by the LPDs in the form of HMS *Fearless* and HMS *Intrepid*, plus the RFA LSLs of the 'Sir' Class. The aircraft carriers can be used but a LPH has been ordered specifically for amphibious operations.

In addition to the conventional vehicles such as Land Rovers and various trucks, the Royal Marines have a number of the Bv206 all-terrain carrier. A few of the previously-operated Volvo Bv202 remain.

Left: Based at Arbroath are the Royal Marines Commacchio Group. Their primary task is the guarding of Britain's nuclear deterrent although they have a number of other taskings.

One of their modes of transport is the Rigid Inflatable Boat (RIB), capable of speeds in the order of 40kts and able to carry six fully equipped commandos.

Right: The Commachios frequently train for their primary role that also can include an anti-terrorist element.

Lower right: The Brigade Patrol Troop of the Royal Marines was formally known as the Mountain and Arctic Warfare Cadre (M&AW Cadre). Its task was the training of Mountain Leaders for the Commandos of 3 Cdo Bde, and as a secondary duty to provide reconnaissance teams for the Commander of 3 Cdo Bde. The M&AW Cadre was well armed with personal weapons but was not intended as an offensive force, being a relatively small unit with intelligence gathering as its war role.

Once over the Drop Zone (DZ) it is important that troops leave the aircraft as quickly as possible to ensure that they land close together. They will then be able to locate each other swiftly and increase their chance of survival. With the red jump light turned to green, the Loadmaster can be seen here assisting the troops to exit rapidly from an RAF Hercules.

Far left: Besides the RIBs, the Commachios are equipped with the Rigid Raider that has a longer range but a lower speed, and cannot carry as many troops.

Left: Some of the Commachio Group are trained and kitted-out with specialist diving equipment to enable them to approach an objective underwater and undetected. Their breathing equipment utilises an oxygen-based gas with a special re-breather system that prevents any tell-tale air bubbles venting to the surface and giving them away.

Left: Once on the ground it is vital that the troops quickly sort their equipment, hide their parachutes and keep a lookout for any enemy to maintain their element of surprise.

Depending on the terrain, the Royal Marines Brigade Patrol Troop are trained to utilise their skiing ability and can cover large distances in a relatively short period.

Currently 3 Cdo Bde is seen as a trouble shooting force with the capability of being sent at short notice to areas of tension anywhere in the world. Its quality of self-reliance has meant that in its role of the M&AW Cadre it should be able to provide a broader reconnaissance capability. This is achieved by enlarging its strength to enable it to be deployed forward of the main force and to keep the Brigade Commander fully briefed.

Below: Depending on the terrain and the objective, the patrol also may be required to continue on foot. To reflect the more global role of the M&AW Cadre, the title of the unit has been changed to the Brigade Patrol Troop. The Troop has been expanded by three senior NCOs and 12 Marines bringing its strength up to 29 men. This enables the Troop to increase the size of each of its four patrols by two men from the previous four, enabling the patrols to carry the additional monitor-

ing and communication equipment required for this role.

The scenario recently practised has involved the Brigade Patrol Troop working with the Recce Troop of 59 Commando Engineer Squadron, Royal Engineers. Their primary task is to report on potential obstacles and engineer tasks forward of the advancing Brigade, as well as placing obstacles in the path of enemy forces. It is likely that here there is scope for mutually beneficial co-operation.

Above: The role of the Brigade Patrol Troop has resulted in a number of the M16 assault rifles being retained. These are usually fitted with the M203 40mm grenade launcher.

Below left: The Royal Marines have standardised on the 5.56mm SA80 Individual Weapon and Light Support Weapon.

Below right: Due to their role, the Brigade Patrol Troop is unlikely to be involved directly in an assault. However, a sniper can hit a precise target without giving away his location. To undertake this role the sniper is equipped with the Accuracy International L96A1 7.62mm rifle that is fitted with the Schmidt & Bender telescopic sight.

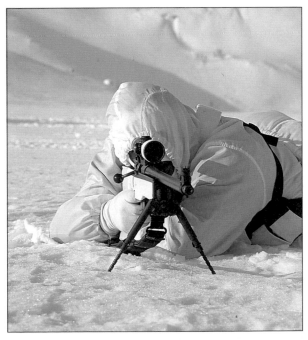

169

Left: Transport for cross-county driving over snow is provided by the Swedish designed and built Bv206. Developed especially for operations in rugged terrain, the vehicle is equally at home on the peat bogs of the Falklands as on the snow of Norway.

The Bv206 comprises of two units linked together by a steering/power link. The front vehicle can accommodate the commander and driver plus three men, while up to 12 more can be fitted into the second unit. The second unit may be used for a range or purposes including that of a field ambulance.

Left: The Royal Marines will operate the Gazelle AH.1 helicopter in all possible theatres of operation and in all conditions.

Left: Currently, the Royal Marines' main transport helicopter is the Lynx AH.7. In addition to the TOW anti-tank missile rails, this Lynx is fitted with skis under the skids for Arctic operations.

The Royal Marines Lynx is basically similar to the Army Lynx AH.7, although there are a few small differences to suit its particular role.

Left: Once at or near the objective, self-preservation becomes vital. In this harsh environment where the wind chill factor can reduce air temperatures to tens of degree below freezing, survival holes must be dug.

Right: Depending on the nature of the exercise, live-firing is conducted in specially designated military training areas. Here Commandos launch a mortar attack onto the objective. However, this firepower is most likely to be implemented by one of the Commandos rather than by the Brigade Patrol Troop.

Left: Currently the Brigade Patrol Troop is continuing with Arctic training — almost anywhere in the world would seem relatively easy after those gruelling conditions in one of the harshest environments. However, insertion by ship, helicopter, aircraft and hovercraft are continually practised, as are parachuting and mountain climbing and long distance cross-country hikes. As new potential threats arise, so the Brigade Patrol Troop will hone its training to that particular environment.

Left: A troop of Royal Marines are deployed by Rigid Raider from the LPD HMS *Fearless* at the start of an amphibious operation.

Left: Depending on the scenario, a number of the Brigade Patrol Troop might be depoloyed ashore to reconoitre and secure the beachhead prior to the main assault.

These are followed up by Marines from one or more of the Commandos in the Landing Craft Vehicle and Personnel (LCVP). Capable of carrying about 30 troops or two small vehicles, the LCVPs can be fitted with a canopy for Arctic operations. Four LCVPs are normally carried by each of the LPDs.

Right: Successive landings would probably include heavier firepower in the form of the Scimitar. These would be carried by the 27.5m Landing Craft Utility (LCU) that are capable of carrying a 60-ton tank or up to 100 troops. Four LCUs are accommodated within the dock area of the LPD during the transit.

Right: Once the landing area is secure, the softer vehicles can be brought ashore from the LSLs. It is probable that at least one Mexiflote pontoon would be carried as part of the equipment required. The LSL is capable of carrying a Mexiflote attached to either side of the hull. Once launched the Mexiflotes can be used to off-load vehicles and equipment from the stern ramp of the LSL.

Right: It is possible that an airstrip might be captured, or constructed, from which the Hercules transport aircraft could operate, in which case the loads would be prepared by members of the Mobile Air Operations Team (MAOT). Their role is to ensure that the loads are safe and secure for further airlifting by the Sea Kings to where they are needed.

Left: With the operation complete, the whole force would withdraw in a controlled fashion to maintain the security of the area. The Royal Marines are the one force that makes maximum use of land, sea and air power.

Right: While this was a fictitious humanitarian exercise, the scenario is very real and is regularly practised by units from all three services. In 1991 members of 3 Cdo Bde were deployed to Northern Iraq to protect the Kurdish refugees. They were suffering from continuing attacks by Saddam Hussein's Revolutionary Guard after Iraq's defeat by the Allied forces. Their next task was rescue work following the Bangladeshi cyclone.

With the world a less stable place now than it has been for many years, this capability of the Royal Marines soon may be required for real to protect British citizens.

In 1994 members of the Royals Marines were deployed to the Gulf following deployment of Iraqi troops along the Kuwait border.

Naval Air Command

The history of Royal Navy flying commenced with the training of the first four naval pilots at Eastchurch on the Isle of Sheppey in 1911. Although the Admiralty favoured the airship, developments with aircraft led to a naval wing within the Royal Flying Corps (RFC) in May 1912. The Royal Naval Air Service (RNAS) was not formed until July 1914, entering World War 1 with just 39 aeroplanes, 52 seaplanes (of which only half were operational) and 6 airships – the RNAS was hardly a force to be reckoned with. However, the destruction of the first Zeppelin by Flight Sub-Lt Warneford over Ostend earned him the first Victoria Cross for the RNAS. Later, during the Dardanelles campaign the first aerial torpedo was dropped successfully from a Short 184.

On 1 April 1918 the RNAS and RFC were amalgamated to form the Royal Air Force. It was not until April 1924 that the Fleet Air Arm (FAA) of the RAF came into being. Then naval officers were given an RAF rank as well as their naval one. In May 1939 the Admiralty regained administrative control once again.

Despite the strides that had been made, the old fashioned dogma in the Admiralty considered that an enemy could only be effectively attacked within the range of guns. Again, the FAA was poorly equipped for the outbreak of war, but it was a heroic action that was to start the change in attitudes. On 11 November 1940, 21 obsolete Fairey Swordfish biplane torpedo bombers took off from HMS *Illustrious*. Although one had to turn back, the rest of the force flew 170 miles and attacked the Italian battle fleet anchored safely behind the powerful defences at Taranto in southern Italy. This action, in which the Italian fleet was crippled by such a relatively small force, was to have a major impact on the outcome of the war.

Through the skill and determination of the officers and men of the FAA, the list of achievements continued and at last recognition was deservedly granted. By the end of World War 2 the FAA had grown from 340 operational aircraft to 1,300 and comprised 70,000 officers and men.

The FAA has continued to grow in stature ever since. Only one year after the end of World War 2 the first ever deck landing of a jet was made, followed the next year by the first landing by a helicopter on a naval vessel at sea. As a world leader in aircraft carrier technology, the FAA introduced the steam catapult, angled deck and the mirror landing sight; and later the first landing of a VTOL aircraft on a carrier deck. With these developments the weight and capabilities of the aircraft increased through the

Right: The Scottish Aviation (BAe) Jetstream T.2 is the military trainer variant of the commuter light transport aircraft, of 14 which were transferred from an RAF order to the Royal Navy. They have been used as navigational and observer trainers to replace the elderly Hunting Percival Sea Prince. Jetstream T.2s are operated by 750 Squadron at RNAS Culdrose.

The Royal Navy subsequently ordered four Jetstream T.3s from BAe (Scottish Aviation having been taken over by BAe) for use in the communication role. Three of the aircraft are based at RNAS Yeovilton and operated by Naval Air Command Operational Sup-

port Flight (NACOSF) – better known as Heron Flight; the fourth is held in reserve. These aircraft are tasked through Flag Officer Navl Aviation (FONA) and used to fly anything from VVIPs to freight throughout Europe.

Sea Hawk and the Scimitar, to the Buccaneer and the Phantom.

But the paying-off of the Royal Navy's aircraft carriers saw the introduction of a new class of ship – the Through Deck Cruiser. Designed to operate the revolutionary V/STOL Sea Harrier, this ship no longer needed the catapults, arrester wires or angled deck because this aircraft could take off and land like a helicopter.

While the first of the new Through Deck Cruisers was being built, a Royal Navy officer, Lt-Cdr Taylor, formulated a theory: he calculated that the Sea Harrier's performance could be greatly enhanced by using a ramp for take-off. Following trials of the ramp, it was discovered that its use enabled the Sea Harrier to carry an extra 1,500lb of fuel or weapons. As a result, all three 'Invincible' Class ships, as they were to become known (and including HMS *Hermes*) were modified to incorporate a 'ski-ramp'.

In 1982 the FAA was plunged into an unexpected war 8,000 miles from home when Argentina invaded the Falkland Islands in the South Atlantic. Up until then, Britain had been reducing its overseas commitments and had become reliant on the broad 'safety blanket' of NATO. The military problem was that the nearest 'safe' location to the Falklands was the small island of Ascension, still some 4,000 miles from the theatre of operations. In the resulting Operation 'Corporate', as it became known, the Royal Navy sent a Task Force to the South Atlantic that needed to be self sufficient and have the capability of regaining the Islands.

A total of 171 naval aircraft in 15 squadrons were deployed. The FAA's Sea Harriers were outnumbered 6:1 by the Argentinians who had the added advantage of operating from land bases. The Sea Harriers flew some 2,000 operational sorties during which 23 enemy aircraft were shot down and many attacks made against ship and shore targets, before the Islands were successfully retaken.

Currently the FAA comprises some 7,500 personnel – or 14 per cent of the total Royal Navy strength – and operates over 300 fixed-wing aircraft and helicopters. All warships from frigate size upwards carry at least one helicopter, with others embarked on some of the RFAs. At the time of writing the FAA is in the process in a mid-life upgrade of virtually all of its current frontline aircraft. This will ensure they are fully effective for many years to come.

Eagerly awaited is the arrival of the EH101 Merlin helicopter. This is the result of a collaborative project between Westland Helicopters and the Italian Agusta company, to produce a helicopter that will eventually replace the Sea King for the Italian and British Navies. In 1991 the British government declared the IBM/Westland combine to be the prime contractor and an order for 44 aircraft was placed for the Royal Navy with delivery planned for 1995 onwards.

The Merlin is powered by three RTM-322 engines that will give it a speed of 167kts at up to 14,288kg maximum all-up weight. A large helicopter with a rotor diameter of 18.6m and an overall length of 22.8m, much use has been made of composite materials to keep the weight down. One of its design

Left: The BAe update to the Sea Harrier force includes the Blue Vixen lookdown/shoot-down radar, and the capability to operate the AMRAAM (Advanced Medium Range Air-to-Air Missile) to replace the long-lived Sidewinder. Eventually all FRS1s will have been converted to these standards.

criteria was a capability to operate in the inhospitable conditions of the North Sea. As a result the Merlin can land on ships in a Sea State 5 with 45kt winds, for which a hauldown and rapid securing device is fitted.

The revolutionary BAe Sea Harrier is a single-seat Vertical/Short Take-Off and Landing (V/STOL) strike fighter with a secondary role of reconnaissance. It was developed from the RAF Harrier family.

Prior to the Falklands War the Harrier/Sea Harrier had a mediocre reputation – even considered in some quarters as something of a gimmick. By the end of the Falklands War this reputation had, deservedly, changed for the better. Although the Sea Harrier was a subsonic aircraft, it had repeatedly entered combat with high performance subsonic A-4 Skyhawks and supersonic Mirages of the Argentinian Air Force and Navy. This resulted in at least 23 Argentinian aircraft being destroyed during air-to-air combat. A total of 28 Sea Harriers from an overall force of 32 aircraft were deployed down in the South Atlantic, where they maintained a 90 per cent availability rate, while still flying some 2,000 operational sorties.

An idea that was utilised for the first time during the Falklands War was the use of merchant ships to operate the Sea Harrier. Although the MV *Atlantic Conveyor* was used only to transport Sea Harriers and helicopters down to the South Atlantic, the principle was established that V/STOL jet fighters could be flown operationally from this type of merchant vessel. It was fortunate that they had already departed when the ship was hit by an Exocet missile, fired by an Argentinian Super Etendard, which caused the loss of the stowed equipment and most of the embarked helicopters.

BAe is currently providing the mid-life update to the Sea Harrier fleet which will result in the aircraft being redesignated Sea Harrier FA.2. Orders have also been placed for 18 additional Sea Harrier FA.2s for delivery from 1995 onwards.

Four ex-RAF Harrier T.4 two-seat trainers are based at RNAS Yeovilton for use by 899 Squadron during pilot conversion training. Each of these aircraft is being converted to T.8 standard to make them fully compatible with the Sea Harrier FA.2.

The Gazelle was one of three helicopter designs which resulted from an Anglo/French collaborative

Right: The Hunter first flew in 1951 and continues to serve with the Royal Navy. A few Hunter GA11s and T8s remain with the Fleet Requirements Air Direction Unit (FRADU), based at RNAS Yeovilton. They are maintained and flown by Flight Refuelling Ltd to provide simulated targets for ships' weapon system training as 'missiles' fired from the Falcon 'mother ship'. The Hunter is now due for retirement and is being replaced by surplus RAF Hawks

Right: A total of 30 Gazelle HT.2s were ordered for the Royal Navy and are operated by 705 Squadron for pilot training at RNAS Culdrose.

deal of the late 1960s, in which the aim was to design and build helicopters for the armed forces of both countries. Three main variants of the Gazelle were built for the British military, of which the AH.1 was the most numerous. This version was designed for operational use by the Army and a few models were supplied to the Royal Marines. The HT.2 was destined for the Royal Navy, while the HT.3 was for the RAF.

The Lynx was the second part of the Anglo-French co-operation package to build three military helicopters (the third being the RAF Puma). Design leadership for the Lynx rested with Westland, while that for the Gazelle and the Puma lay with Aerospatiale.

Two variants of the Lynx were originally built for the British Armed Forces: the AH.1 was for the Army, although the Royal Marines also took delivery of a number. The second variant was the HAS.2 for the Royal Navy of which 88 were ordered. Both variants have been upgraded and are now redesignated: the AH.1 is now the AH.7., while the HAS.2 has become HAS.3. However, more enhancements have resulted in the latter being further redesignated HAS.8.

The Westland Lynx HAS.2 entered service with 700L Squadron at RNAS Yeovilton in September 1976 for trials purposes. 702 Squadron was the next unit to operate the Lynx when it commissioned in January 1978 at RNAS Portland.

With the disbanding of 700L Squadron, all the Lynx HAS.2s were based at Portland with either 702 Squadron for training, or with 815 and 829 Squadrons for operational purposes. Many of these Lynxes would be detached to provide the ship's flight aboard various warships. In 1992, 829 Squadron was disbanded and currently all ship's flights are formed by, and parented from, 815 Squadron.

Above: The Lynx is currently undergoing a major systems and airframe upgrading that will equip it to operate aboard Royal Navy ships for many years to come. Redesignated Lynx HAS.8, these changes include the fitting of new rotor blades that provide a 30 per cent increase in lift over the previous ones; other enhancements include the fitting of the Racal Avionics Tactical Management System and GEC Sea Owl Passive Identification System.

Below: The most numerous helicopter type within the Royal Navy, the primary role of the Sea King HAS.6 is ASW using the dunking sonar (illustrated) or sonar buoys. They also have an ASV capability. During the Gulf War a pair of Sea Kings were even modified to spot moored mines and spent some time deployed aboard a Dutch Naval vessel.

Designed to search for surface vessels, if required the Lynx HAS.3 can press home an attack using Sea Skua missiles, a combination that proved highly effective against Iraqi shipping during the Gulf War. The Lynx can also assist in the ASW role, or simply for communications purposes when it might be tasked with transferring personnel, mail or even freight.

A development of the American-designed Sikorsky SH-3, the Westland Sea King has been operated in various roles over the years by the Royal Navy. Initially 56 were purchased as the Sea King

Above: Sea King HC.4s of 845 and 848 Squadrons were deployed into Kuwait to support 1st Armoured Division. They were hastily modified to incorporate missile warners, decoy flares, GPS and an improved IFF, as well as being painted pink. Despite the fitting of sand filters, the sand caused some problems with the engines.

Right: In addition to the ASW role, the Sea King has proved to be extremely useful in the Commando support role. Designated HC.4, this variant has a basic Sea King fuselage with a seating capacity for 28 fully-equipped troops. In addition it is capable of lifting over 3,500kg of freight on a single under fuselage hook.

Above: The Sea King is an extremely capable rescue helicopter. Together with the RAF variant, they often appear in the news helping those in distress.

HAS.1 for the ASW role, later improved to the HAS.2 standard. Subsequent modifications resulted in a further redesignation as the HAS.5. This variant has recently completed further enhancements to its capabilities that have resulted in it being redesignated HAS.6. These latest upgrades includes enhancements to the dipping sonar and the processing and communications equipment.

A further main role for the Sea King was one that had not been envisaged for it until the Falklands War. With the scrapping of the conventional aircraft carriers and the retiring of the Fairey Gannet, the Royal Navy lost its Airborne Early Warning (AEW) capability. At the time this was not considered a major problem with the shrinking areas of British responsibilities around the world. It was thought that the Royal Navy would be concentrated in the NATO region where AEW cover would be provided by the

Left: Prospective pilots who have completed the initial interviews and evaluation at RAF College Cranwell, undertake an aptitude assessment at Plymouth/Roborough Airport. This is conducted by Airwork on behalf of the Royal Navy, with civilian instructors flying the Grob G115.D Heron.

During a three-week period students undergo ground school and a total of 13 hours of flying in the Grob. This will take them up to solo standard and enable an aptitude assessment to be made.

Airwork are also contracted to provide another course for rotary-wing pilots who have shown the right aptitude for fast jet training. This retraining course include 22 hours flying the Grob to convert to fixed-wing aircraft. On completion the pilot progresses to Advanced Flying Training (AFT) at RAF Valley, Anglesey.

Left: Those Naval students that have passed the aptitude assessment progress to the Joint Elementary Flying School at RAF Topcliffe, together with RAF students. Here they undertake 62 hours of flying training in the Slingsby Firefly together with ground school on a course run by Huntings.

Most students who successfully complete the course move on to RNAS Culdrose and 705 Squadron. A few successful students who show an aptitude for fast jet flying will progress to the RAF's No 1 FTS at RAF Linton-on-Ouse. Here they are given 130 hours of basic flying training over 43 weeks which includes instruction in ground school, simulators, survival, navigation as well as general aircraft handling and formation flying in the Tucano T.1.

Left: Those selected for fast jet flying will move on to No 4 FTS at RAF Valley where they will receive their Advanced Flying Training (AFT) plus that of the Tactical Weapons Unit (TWU).

Here, the Naval student is strapped into the front seat of an RAF Hawk T.1 of No 74 Squadron prior to undertaking a training sortie.

RAF and other NATO forces from nearby land bases. The Falklands War highlighted the flaw in that plan.

Firstly, Britain was on her own and could not rely on the modern NATO AEW force. The RAF was still awaiting a replacement for its aged Shackleton aircraft which, due to their slow speed and old age, were considered impractical to operate over such long distances to the South Atlantic.

The result was that the Task Force had to rely on the ships' radar for a warning of aerial attack. With tactics now involving low-level flying, this meant a nightmare for those responsible for air defence. When a pair of Argentinian Super Etendards made their low approach and fired their Exocet missiles, there was only a matter of seconds available for their detection. Due to a combination of events, the incoming missiles were not detected in time and resulted in the destruction of HMS *Sheffield.*

While events had been successful up to that point in the Operation, this stark reality vividly brought home the yawning gap in the Navy's capabilities. A hurried programme was implemented to provide some aerial radar coverage and the platform selected was the Sea King. Two HAS.2 airframes were selected, the ASW equipment removed and a modified version of the Searchwater radar fitted, resulting in the Sea King being redesignated AEW.2. Unfortunately, the modification to these Sea Kings was completed too late to provide coverage during Operation 'Corporate', but 849 Squadron now embarks a flight on each of the carriers during any deployment.

At the time of writing, plans are underway to greatly enhance the capability of the Sea King AEW.2 with new avionics, improved aerial and waveguide designs, enhanced transmitter performance, communications, IFF and JTIDS. Further roles for the Sea King include crew training and SAR.

Prospective pilots who have completed the initial interviews and evaluation at RAF College Cranwell, undertake an aptitude assessment at Plymouth/Roborough Airport. This is conducted by Airwork on behalf of the Royal Navy, with civilian instructors flying the Grob G115.D Heron.

Left: The fast jet student then joins 899 Squadron for conversion onto the Sea Harrier. In addition to the ground school and simulator work the pilot will fly some 30 hours in the Harrier T.4N. A further 60 hours of flying training will be carried out on the Sea Harrier FRS.2. Once this has been completed the few pilots that have successfully completed the course will be posted to one of the operational squadrons, 800 or 801.

Left: 702 Naval Air Squadron was originally formed in 1936, today the squadron is based at RNAS Portland where its role is to train all Lynx aircrew and maintenance ratings. To undertake this role, the squadron is equipped with 12 Lynx HAS.3s and a complement of over 130 officers and men.

Student aircrew are posted to 702 Squadron from 705 Squadron at RNAS Culdrose. For the next six months they are taught how to fly the Lynx in its primary roles of ASV and ASW. To this is added the secondary roles of naval gunfire support, SAR, troop lifting, communications flying and VERTREP.

Once the aircrew or maintainers have reached the necessary standard and completed the course, they can be posted to 815 Squadron and then on to a ship's flight aboard a warship.

Left: 705 Naval Air Squadron, was formed in 1936 from part of 444 (Catapult) Flight. Today 705 Squadron is based at RNAS Culdrose where it teaches naval aircrew students the art of flying helicopters. The squadron has a strength of 24 officers and ratings and is equipped with 19 Gazelle HT.2s that are maintained by Hunting.

Approximately 90 Royal Navy students a year will complete this course. 705 Squadron also undertakes annually the basic training of 15 students from the German Navy.

Lower left: 706 Naval Air Squadron was originally formed in Australia on 6 March 1945 to train aircrew for the British Pacific Fleet, today the squadron has returned to the training role and operates 12 Sea King HAS.5/6s from RNAS Culdrose. Course student aircrew join the squadron from 705 Squadron, together with some experienced fixed-wing pilots for type conversion. The Squadron has a total strength of 170 officers and ratings and is equipped with 11 Sea Kings HAS.5/6s.

The role of 706 Squadron is to provide advanced training for pilots, observers and aircrewmen in anti-submarine warfare. A secondary role for the squadron is to assist 771 Squadron in the role of long range SAR for the South West Region of the United Kingdom and the South Western Approaches.

Right: 707 Naval Air Squadron was formed on 22 April 1945, the squadron currently trains pilots and crew to fly the Sea King HC.4 at RNAS Yeovilton. In addition to the training role, a few of 707 Squadron's experienced crews fly some of the security tasks in Northern Ireland. The Squadron has a strength of 150 officers and ratings and is equipped with 8 Sea King HC.4s.

Centre right: 750 Naval Air Squadron was formed in 1939 with the Blackburn Shark and Hawker Osprey. Currently it is equipped with the Jetstream T.2 that it operates from RNAS Culdrose to provide basic flying training for Royal Navy observers. To fulfil this role the squadron has a strength of 50 officers and ratings together with 13 Jetsream T.2s maintained by Hunting.

The Observers' course lasts six months during which time they will be taught radar handling, plus high and low level navigation techniques. This will include all aspects of aviation including safety awareness and various other tasks to enable the observer to fulfil the role of navigator. Once completed the qualified student will proceed to 702 or 706 Squadron for type conversion.

Right: 771 Naval Air Squadron was formed on 24 May 1939 at RNAS Portland with the Fairey Swordfish, 771 Squadron is now based at RNAS Culdrose where its primary responsibility is the rescue of crashed military aircrew. Fortunately, military accidents are rare these days and the bulk of the squadron's work is provided by its secondary role of providing assistance to civil incidents – usually through HM Coastguard. Equipped with 5 Sea Kings HAS.5 (SAR), 771 Squadron comprises of nine pilots, two observers, five divers and five aircrewmen, together with a maintenance team. Between them they keep a 24hr coverage 365 days of the year. One Sea King is kept on 15mins notice by day and 45mins at night, although in practice the aircraft is usually airborne within 4mins. Emergency calls can result in a Sea King being flown 200 miles out to sea, to lift an injured seaman from a small fishing vessel in a Force 8 gale. More common during the summer months is the rescue of stranded holidaymakers.

Below: 772 Naval Air Squadron was formed on 28 September 1939 with Fairey Swordfish from a detachment of 771 Squadron at Portland. Currently the squadron is equipped with the Sea King HC.4 and is based at RNAS Portland. The primary role of the squadron is to provide a SAR capability for the South Coast from Bournemouth to Start Point in Devon. 772 Squadron comprises of 110 officers and ratings plus 6 Sea King HC.4s.

The Sea King HC.4 used by 772 Squadron is the standard troop carrying helicopter but carries an extra aircrewman, usually a qualified SAR diver, and if required a medical assistant or doctor. One Sea King and crew are always kept on 15mins readiness from dawn to dusk, 365 days a year.

A secondary role for the squadron is to provide sea transfers for British and NATO personnel aboard ships in the Portland training area. It will also pro-vide aircraft for personnel undergoing training at Portland in flight deck operations and helicopter training. Included are VIP transfers, torpedo recovery, RNLI training and airborne photography, among many other military tasks. With the moving of the Portland sea training facilities to Devonport, this part of their role will cease.

Below: 800 Naval Air Squadron was formed on 2 May 1933 with the Hawker Nimrod and Osprey. On 23 April 1980 the squadron became the first to re-equip with the Sea Harrier FRS.1 and then the first to operationally deploy onto a carrier when it embarked aboard HMS *Invincible.*

The home base for 800 Squadron is RNAS Yeovilton and the squadron embarks aboard *Invincible* when she is deployed operationally. The squadron is manned by 100 officers and men and is now equipped with six Sea Harrier FA.2.s.

During the Falklands War the squadron was embarked aboard *Hermes,* tasked with high and low-level bombing, long-range probe and strafing, besides the normal roles of CAP and recce. A total of 13 Argentinian aircraft were destroyed during air-to-air combat by 800 Squadron.

Right: 801 Naval Air Squadron was formed in May 1933 as a Fleet Fighter Squadron, and is currently equipped with the Sea Harrier FA.2 with its home base at RNAS Yeovilton. When deployed, the squadron embarks aboard *Ark Royal* to provide CAP, recce and strike capability for the Carrier Group. 801 Squadron is manned by 100 officers and men plus six Sea Harrier FA.2s.

Centre right: 810 Naval Air Squadron First formed in 1938 with 12 Fairey Swordfish aboard HMS *Hermes*, today 810 Squadron is based at RNAS Culdrose with the Sea King HAS6 for anti-submarine warfare. The squadron consists of nearly 200 officers and men plus 10 Sea King HAS.6.

810 Squadron provides a 22-week operational training course for pilot, observer and aircrew before they join a frontline squadron. During this time they may be detached to Portland for operational ASW training sorties. Here they will also be trained in deck landings and load lifting with further sea training aboard RFA *Argus* or other available RFAs.

Lower right: Formed in November 1938, 814 Squadron is currently equipped with the Sea King HAS.6 and has its home base at RNAS Culdrose. The squadron's primary role is to provide anti-submarine protection for HMS *Invincible* and the rest of her convoy or Task Force. The squadron has a complement of 170 officers and men plus seven Sea King HAS6s.

The secondary roles of 814 Squadron include surveillance, troop and tactical transport, VERTREP and CASEVAC. When deployed, the squadron often responds to SAR requests.

Because HMS *Invincible* is part of the UK Amphibious Force, 814 Squadron might well be tasked with carrying underslung loads ashore. The squadron can also be re-roled to carry 17 fully armed troops or up to nine stretches in the air ambulance role.

Above: When 815 Squadron was formed in 1939 it was equipped with the Fairey Swordfish for the torpedo attack role. Today, the squadron continues in this role operating the Lynx HAS.3, equipped with torpedoes and depth-charges for ASW, and Sea Skua for the ASV role. 815 Squadron comprises 480 officers and men and is equipped with some 45 Lynx HAS.3s making it the largest helicopter squadron in Europe.

The squadron is based at RNAS Portland but provides the aircrew and maintenance ratings for all the embarked Lynx flights aboard frigates, destroyers and HMS *Endurance*. There are approximately 50 ship's flights, but not all are operational simultaneously.

Below left: 819 Naval Air Squadron was formed in 1940 with the Fairey Swordfish. Today the squadron in based at RNAS Prestwick from where it flies the Sea King HAS.6. Its primary role is to provide anti-submarine protection for the Clyde submarine base at Faslane. The squadron is also tasked with providing SAR in an area that features rough seas, a hazardous coastline and mountains, all of which contribute in a big way to the squadron's SAR duties.

When 826 Squadron was disbanded in 1993, its Sea Kings and aircrew were absorbed into an expanded 819 Squadron. They will now provide Sea Kings and crew to operate aboard the Type 22 frigates and RFA patrols.

To fulfil these functions, 819 Squadron has 250 officers and men plus eight Sea King HAS.6s.

Right: First formed in April 1933, today 820 Squadron is equipped with the Sea King HAS.6 and normally deploys aboard HMS *Ark Royal*, but may be carried by RFA ships when required. From here the Sea King HAS.6 is operated to provide anti-submarine protection. The squadron comprises 183 officers and men, plus seven Sea King HAS.6s, and is based at RNAS Culdrose when not embarked.

In April 1982, 824 Squadron was embarked aboard *Invincible* and deployed to the South Atlantic as part of the Task Force. During the conflict over 4,700hrs were flown including the VERTREP of some 1,200 tons of stores.

Below: In February 1943, 845 Squadron was formed as a torpedo, bomber and reconnaissance squadron equipped with the Grumman Avenger. Today the squadron flies the Sea King HC4 and has its home at RNAS Yeovilton. However, operations and training exercises see the squadron deployed to many locations and ships. The squadron comprises 150 officers and men plus seven Sea King HC.4s.

The primary role of 845 Squadron is support of the Royal Marines of 3 Cdo Bde. Exercises have frequently taken place in the inhospitable Arctic condi-

tions of Norway during training for the protection of NATO's Northern Flank. However, the emphasis on extreme cold weather training is being altered following the break-up of the Soviet Union and the Warsaw Pact.

In 1982 the squadron was deployed to the Falklands where it provided a valuable capability to the Task Force. With the Gulf War in 1991, the squadron

was deployed to Saudi Arabia in support of 1st Armoured Division for action in Kuwait and Iraq. In 1992, 845 Squadron's B Flight was deployed to Croatia to operate in support of the British forces assisting the UN humanitarian relief operation. Besides providing CASEVAC for the British soldiers, they are frequently involved in transferring civilian refugees and casualties for treatment.

Below: 849 Naval Air Squadron was formed on 1 August 1943 with the Grumman Avenger. Today the squadron provides the Royal Navy with an AEW capability with its Sea King AEW.2s. The squadron has its HQ at RNAS Culdrose and is made up of two three-helicopter flights which deploy aboard the operational carriers, plus an HQ Flight. The total strength of 849 Squadron is 124 officers and men plus 8 Sea King AEW.2s.

Opposite page, top: 899 Naval Air Squadron formed on 15 December 1942 with Supermarine Seafires. Today the squadron operates the eight Sea Harrier FA.2s and four Harrier T4.Ns from RNAS Yeovilton and is manned by 110 officers and men.

Above: 846 Naval Air Squadron was formed on 1 April 1943 with the Grumman Avenger. Today the squadron is based at RNAS Yeovilton with the Sea King HC4 but, like 845 Squadron, it spends much of its time away on exercises and deployments. 846 Squadron comprises of 150 officers and men plus eight Sea King HC.4s.

Since 1979, the squadron has operated the Sea King HC.4 in support of 3 Cdo Bde. With a useful troop-carrying capability, the Sea Kings always play an integral part in Royal Marine amphibious landings and other exercises.

In 1982, 846 Squadron was heavily involved in the Falklands War where it flew some 2,800hrs. Later, it was also involved in the withdrawal of British and other nationals from war-torn Beirut. In 1990, 846 Squadron was deployed to the Gulf and during the six weeks of the war flew some 1,200hrs during which time it never missed a single operational sortie.

Only 11 days after returning home, 846 Squadron was deployed to Northern Iraq as part of the multi-national force that was sent to ease the plight of the Kurdish people. During that three-month deployment, a total of 1,100hrs were flown with no operational sorties lost. Meanwhile, 846 Squadron's A Flight was in Bangladesh aboard RFA Fort Grange where it provided air support to the hurricane-struck region.

Apart from its primary peacetime role of pilot and engineer training for the Sea Harrier squadrons, 899 Squadron carries out trials of new associated equipment and conducts specialised courses to increase further the capabilities of the highly experienced aircrew. Although it is a training squadron, 899 also has an operational squadron number and during a period of tension it could undergo a swift transition to a fully operational squadron. During 1982, 899 Squadron made such a transition and was deployed with the Task Force during the Falklands War. During this action three members of the squadron were awarded Distinguished Service Cross for gallantry.

Right: The Heron Flight was originally the name of the station flight for RNAS Yeovilton. When the communications squadron (781 Squadron) disbanded many of Sea Herons were absorbed into Heron Flight and its communications role expanded accordingly. Today Heron Flight is equipped with three Jestream T.3 and a Gazelle HT.2.

Also incorporated within Heron Flight is the Royal Navy Historic Flight. The Flight comprises of a pair of Fairey Swordfish, one painted in 836 Squadron markings while the other is painted to represent 810 Torpedo Spotting Squadron. The third airworthy member of the Flight is a Fairey Firefly painted in the Korean War markings of 812 Squadron. These historic aircraft appears at many events throughout the country during the summer season.

Further aircraft on the strength of the Historic Flight are a Sea Hawk, Sea Fury FB.II, Sea Fury T.22 and Chipmunk T.10. The Chipmunk is used as a crew trainer and the Sea Fury FB.II is undergoing long term refurbishment to flying condition. The damaged Sea Fury TT.20 is on

loan from the RAF and the Sea Hawk has not flown for a number of years

Sadly, the Historic Flight receives no financial assistance from the MoD and has to be self supporting. As a result the

Swordfish Heritage Trust has been established to raise the necessary funds. For those interested in helping, details can be obtained from the CO, Royal Navy Historic Flight at Yeovilton.

Royal Naval Reserve

The Royal Naval Reserve (RNR) comprises of nearly 4,000 volunteer men and women from all walks of life who enjoy giving some of their spare time to the Royal Navy. Approximately 1,500 of these men and women have served in the Royal Navy before joining the RNR. They meet for one or two nights per week for training, and once a year spend a week at sea putting this training into practice.

In 1994 the RNR was restructured to reflect the Royal Navy's new requirements following the collapse of the Warsaw Pact and the reduction in East-West tension. Some roles that have been provided by the RNR are no longer required, but others have needed expanding.

The RNR now operates from 13 Reserve Training Centres that are strategically placed throughout the country. Although the RNR-manned MCMV vessels have been withdrawn there are still opportunities to go to sea, with many different areas of specialisation and the opportunity to train in a variety of types of Royal Navy ships and auxiliary vessels. The benefit for the Royal Navy is that this will enable a rapid build-up and augmentation of its forces in time of crisis and conflict.

Opposite page, top: Members of the RNR can now fulfil their role by undertaking tasks on a variety of Royal Navy frontline warships. The RNR of the 1990s has seven core roles – Operations, Logistics, Defence Intelligence, Interrogation, Public Affairs, Medical and Air.

The Operational role is by far the largest, providing personnel to serve afloat and as HQ staff ashore. As seamen afloat they might be communicators, amphibious warfare and minewarfare specialists; alternatively, ashore they could be officers and ratings working in submarine operations management, navigational warnings, intelligence, naval control of merchant shipping or generally assisting in the operational control of the Royal Navy.

Opposite page, bottom: The RNR provides HQ staff down in the bunker of the Operation Control Room (OCR) of the Fleet HQ at Northwood, Middlesex.

Right: The Submarine Operations Room for the NATO COMSUBEASTLANT being manned by members of the RNR ...

Below: ... as is the NATO Radio Room where signals are transmitted and received.

The Logistics role is a new one for the RNR, but will draw on the expertise of the clerks, stores accountants and cooks who were previously supporting the RNR minesweepers. It covers the provision of food, fuel and transport to the Royal Navy at specified sites in the UK or abroad.

The Air role is exclusive to ex-Royal Navy aircrew, ground and maintenance crews due to the level of specialised training required. These servicemen and women will have volunteered to join the RNR after completion of their period of regular service. Due to the nature of the work, the Air Branch has always worked alongside its regular counterparts.

Above: RNR Air Branch includes aircrew instructors, flying here with 702 Squadron on the Lynx ...

Left: ... Lynx simulator instructors...

Left: ... and can include operational pilots such as these with 772 Squadron...

Lower left: ... and air traffic controllers.

The other RNR roles will not need the same number of reservists as these previously required, but will require their members to be specialists in their field.

These changes are to ensure that the Royal Navy and the Royal Naval Reserve move forward together, to ensure that they are able to meet any future threat quickly and efficiently. The fact that the reservists will be able to train and work alongside their regular counterparts will enable better levels of understanding and trust, to the benefit of all concerned. To the RNR, there is now also the benefit of training on a wide range of ships.

Over the years the RNR has provided a valuable source of expertise and trained manpower, particularly during World War 2 when large numbers of reservists served with bravery and courage. The traditions that have evolved since then will ensure that the commitment and dedication of present and future members of the RNR will continue. As a result the RNR will remain to be a valued part of the UK's defence and security.